CONCEPTUALISING MAN AND SOCIETY

CONCEPTUALISING MAN AND SOCIETY

Perspectives in Early Indian Sociology

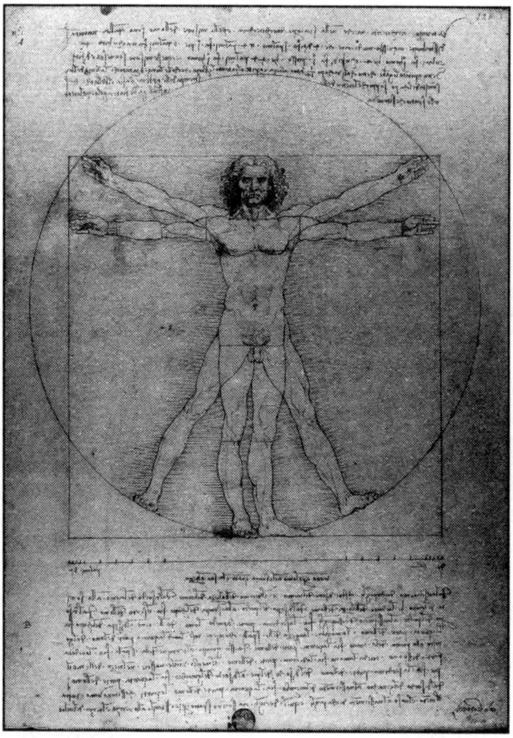

PRADIP KUMAR BOSE

Orient BlackSwan

CONCEPTUALISING MAN AND SOCIETY: PERSPECTIVES IN EARLY INDIAN SOCIOLOGY

ORIENT BLACKSWAN PRIVATE LIMITED

Registered Office
3-6-752 Himayatnagar, Hyderabad 500 029, Telangana, India
e-mail: centraloffice@orientblackswan.com

Other Offices
Bengaluru, Bhopal, Chennai, Guwahati, Hyderabad, Jaipur, Kolkata, Lucknow, Mumbai, New Delhi, Noida, Patna, Vijayawada

ISBN 978-93-5287-283-1

027391

Typeset in
Book Antiqua 10.5/12.6
by Le Studio Graphique, Gurgaon 122 001

Printed in India at
Glorious Printers, Delhi

Published by
Orient Blackswan Private Limited
3-6-752, Himayatnagar, Hyderabad 500 029
e-mail: info@orientblackswan.com

To the memory of my mother

Kamala Bose

1922–2006

CONTENTS

INTRODUCTION

> A phrase by Marx is pertinent here: man produces man. How should it be understood? In my judgement, what ought to be produced is not man as nature supposedly designed him, or as his essence ordains him to be—we need to produce something that doesn't exist yet, without being able to know what it will be. (Foucault 2000: 275)

The colonial connection of Indian social science shaped the ideological nuances towards the growth of related disciplines, particularly sociology and anthropology. In its formative years Indian sociology displayed two distinctive characteristics: first, its appropriation of the colonial discourse; and second, the opposite tendency of criticising and rejecting Western categories of knowledge. A careful perusal of early history of Indian sociology shows that one strand of it was influenced by the principles and logic of colonial knowledge and nineteenth-century orientalist 'historical' explanations. At the same time, there was a different tendency which was critical of the application of methods, categories and concepts of Western origin for the study of a historically and culturally distinct entity such as Indian society. This book describes sociological and anthropological approaches to the study of society in India and attempts to demonstrate the contrary tendencies in the writings of early sociologists of India.

The contradictory approaches to the study of Indian society lead to one of the fundamental problems of Indian sociology, namely, its quest for indigenisation, to discover the roots of sociology in Indian social reality and tradition. Early Indian sociologists encountered influential Western doctrines of the utilitarian thinkers who pointed out basic institutional faults in the Indian social systems calling for fundamental reforms. The implied ideology of the utilitarian-rationalist theory proclaimed the notion of 'progress' and 'unilinear evolutionism', which ultimately tended to place Indian society very low in the evolutionary hierarchy. This was viewed by many sociologists as an ideological interpretation of India which placed it in a relationship of cultural inferiority and dependence. These sociologists, therefore, rejected this thesis and in the process, were unwilling to accept the particular variety of sociology which was based on nominalistic philosophical assumptions about the nature of society. This model began with the individual as the fundamental unit of social structure, which in aggregate expressed its main attribute. The essays in this book show that both Radhakamal Mukerjee and D. P. Mukerji were serious critics of individualism who argued that the Western notion of the individual has no relevance for the understanding of the Indian social structure. Thus, attempts were made from the very beginning to introduce Indian categories or conceptual systems into their interpretation of Indian society.

Early Indian sociologists expressed interest in larger sociological and philosophical issues like the concepts of tradition, values, community, person and personality and most importantly, on the conceptualisation of man, which eventually was abolished by later generations of sociologists from the theoretic construct of Indian sociology. The early sociologists considered these concepts not as abstractions but as a substantive part of Indian social reality. Interest in such concepts arose because these sociologists questioned the relevance of Western concepts for Indian society. D. P. Mukerji criticised the Parsonian assumption of 'actor-situation' because he believed that the unit of the Indian social system is *not* the individual as actor and that action for the Indian cannot be considered as individualistic in the sense Parsons describes. He argues that action for the Indian is 'inherently structured on a normative, teleological' matrix, and not on a 'voluntaristic system of coordinates' (Mukerji 2002 [1958]: 267). Louis Dumont later echoed Mukerji's thesis when he denied the existence of the 'individual' as a category in Indian tradition (Dumont 1970 [1966]).

The characteristics of early sociological enterprise, especially by Radhakamal and Dhurjati Prasad, were the employment of a philosophical approach towards understanding of social science. Radhakamal Mukerjee believed that philosophy constitutes the matrix of every science, providing its presuppositions and first principles. But for social science philosophy becomes especially significant because its axioms, assumptions and principles must be clarified, tested and validated by philosophy. Mukerjee writes: 'Philosophy always governs as it reflects social meanings, attitudes and values. Out of a floating mass of intellectual and social traditions, values and aspirations, philosophy selects, rejects, integrates or exaggerates some as essential conditions to a liberal and humane way of life' (Mukerjee 2005b [1960]: 51). In his Presidential Address to the Indian Sociological Society in 1955, D. P. Mukerji points out that development in the social sciences is illustrated by the search for: a) basic concepts like status, mobility, community, conflict, etc.; b) some common methodological principles; and c) a philosophical approach. However, he adds: 'The popularity of a method is often dependent on academic fashion [and] the philosophical approach is at present out of court' (Mukerji 2002 [1958]: 263). Early critiques of the individual and a search for alternative concepts of man consistent with Indian reality were products of such philosophical exercise. With the emergence of empirical sociology, the socio-philosophical approach took a back seat. In the same Presidential Address, Mukerji laments:

> I suspect that in the course of its 'flight from philosophy', which is almost always used pejoratively in these days,

> scientific social research has been hopelessly dispersed. As an Indian, I find it impossible to discover any life-meaning in the jungle of the so-called empirical social research monographs. While statistics seek to give some sort of precision in trends, precision becomes non-significant in the absence of any theory and direction. In India, the danger arising out of the aversion from 'philosophy' is much less than in Europe or the USA, though I am not sure how long it will remain so under the high-powered pressure of modern academic fashion. (Mukerji 2002 [1958]: 264–265)

We will come to the question of 'scientific', value-free, empirical social science research in the context of our discussion of Ramkrishna Mukherjee in greater detail, but before that a few more points about the sociologists of Lucknow University. It is often argued that these sociologists were interested in the integration of select conceptual categories of Indian and Western origin (Venugopal 1998: 59–60). However it will be more correct to say that the sociologists who attempted to draw the elements of Indian tradition were actually seeking the rationalisation of tradition or its mere sociological interpretation. As Singh (1983: 18) writes: 'None of such attempts go into the existential phenomenology of man and his problems emerging in the process of the growth of industrial society'. In other words, the problem of integration is a complex one and often depends upon specific cultural traditions and their historicity in a particular society. The essays brought together in this volume are an attempt to grasp some of the ideological issues confronted by the early sociologists in India. The ideological tension in early Indian sociology has been analysed around the concept of man, the individual, person, caste, culture, and methodology. These essays explore the theoretic variations, cognitive and methodological profile of Indian sociology in the process of its early growth.

The other important theme that influenced Indian sociology and social anthropology in this period was the discourse of nationalism. Srinivas and Panini have rightly pointed out that in India, the growth of sociology and social anthropology was intimately influenced by nationalism (1973: 180). Among the early social scientists in India Nirmal Kumar Bose can be considered as one of the best examples of a nationalist social thinker. Bose was a dedicated nationalist and a firm believer in Gandhian ideology; he was incarcerated twice for taking part in the Non-cooperation movement and the Quit India movement, and was a firm believer in India as a unifying idea and concept. Bose privileged culture and history in his method and analysis because he believed that the idea of India can only be demonstrated through the cultural diversity of the nation. His view of caste as a system which was effective in reducing conflict and competition and instrumental in guiding the economic life by a 'moral code' represented the nationalist thinking on caste. In this Bose was following Gandhi who believed that the ideal fourfold *varna* scheme was meant to be a non-competitive functional division of labour. Bose's interest in history, especially the history of temples, was also driven by the nationalist agenda for self-representation, for projecting the nation's past undistorted by foreign interpretations. After Independence when the question of nation-building became paramount, Bose's overriding concern for 'national-unity' in his writings again reproduced the nationalist discourse of a unified India. In the process, however, he ignored the views of those situated at different locations in Indian society who had their own distinct conceptions of the nation.

The post-independent Indian state followed the agenda of nationalist thought and conceived sociology simply as the study of Indian society. The discipline was professionalised and organised within the territory of the nation-state and developed a close relationship with official discourses on nation-state and modernity. Methodological nationalism became the model of the sociological community, who regarded the nation-state as the natural or even necessary form of society in modernity. Methodological nationalism is the naturalisation of the nation-state by the sociologists who assume a synchronous relation between 'society' and the 'nation-state', and conflate the two categories for the purposes of social science. Methodological nationalism represents and reinforces the identification that many sociologists maintain with the nation-state. A major instrument employed by sociologists towards this end was the empirical investigation of various segments of Indian society, and sociologists were exhorted to undertake rigorous empirical work which was usually combined with the undervaluation of theory. The proliferation of village studies in the Fifties and Sixties of the last century demonstrate clearly the shift in the orientation of sociological research.

As a result the broad theoretical landscape of the earlier sociologists disappeared. The sociological insights of the Lucknow School fell into obscurity under the influence of narrow empiricism and excessive stress on 'realistic', field-based study of micro-social institutions. Under the strong influence of such a 'regime of truth' the Lucknow sociologists were considered speculative, conjectural, and blamed wrongly for their reliance on Brahminical and Sanskritic notions of Indian tradition (Oommen 2007). Radhakamal or Dhurjati Prasad could not fashion a school in the epistemological sense. They could not even leave behind a critical mass of students who would follow their path. Beginning from the Fifties, in the next two or three decades of the last century it was really difficult to find any theoretical reflections on man or the individual and society. Yogendra Singh's scholarly and insightful book *Image of Man: Ideology and Theory in Indian Sociology* (1983) remains the sole exception which was written against the tide. In the concluding section of this book we will discuss the reasons for this 'epistemological break' and possible explanations for this obscurity.

When we discuss the rise of empirical sociology in India, it has to be remembered that Ghurye was also an empiricist and believed that 'facts' describe the situation more authentically than any theoretical construction, although the 'facts' on which Ghurye relied so much were produced under the discourse of 'orientalist empiricism'. Ghurye worked under the shadow of colonial discourse which defined the discipline as a body of knowledge that classified, categorised and documented the population under its rule. The significance of orientalism was that as a mode of knowing the other it was a supreme example of the construction of the other, a form of authority.

Consequently, the empirical exercise undertaken by Ghurye represented more a sign of power exerted by the West than a true discourse on India. So, although Ghurye's account of caste and race appears on the surface to be merely a descriptive one, it has a systematic structure and theoretical underpinnings. Ghurye insisted that in India, more intensive empirical investigations are needed before one is able to venture into theoretical constructs; however, his own empirical exercise was bound by colonial epistemological authority.

In the post-Independence era methodological nationalism was combined with empiricist epistemology so that 'scientific' study of society could depend on a neutral and dispassionate observation of the world. Fieldwork and surveys became two major instruments for collection of information to be used not simply for social research, but by the state for the governance of the population. Fieldwork was supposed to be intense, long-term research conducted among the populace, but sociologists and anthropologists were also urged to perform quantitative surveys, textual, demographic and other types of analyses depending upon local conditions and the nature of the research project. Social survey referred to data collection that employed both interviewing and sampling to produce quantitative data-sets and were used to provide descriptive statistics for national, regional or local populations. Though it can be argued that 'the field' is a reified entity and assumptions are made about its unity, cohesiveness, and so on, which renders it problematic in terms of conceptualisation and of its claim as a superior methodology. And in surveys the highly asymmetric power relation between researcher and interviewee is detrimental to the quality of the data collected; they provide a false aura of objectivity which makes their results vulnerable to political manipulation. However, what was acclaimed in these methods was objectivity, value-neutrality, and the scientific quality of the information collected. With the rise of empirical sociology in India, theory was discounted; that knowledge is a product of human reason which established connections and associations between ideas was forgotten.

Ramkrishna Mukherjee's effort to formulate a 'scientific, value-free' methodology for social research has to be understood in this context. Mukherjee belonged to the next generation of sociologists who in his early academic career wrote *The Rise and Fall of the East India Company* (1958), which was basically a sociologist's interpretation of social history. However, beginning from 1975, for the next twenty years he occupied himself with developing and perfecting a methodology that he called the 'inductive-inferential' method of social research. As the essay in this volume shows, this was a futile effort full of contradictions and inconsistencies. However, as D. P. Mukerji would have said, the popularity of a method is often dependent on academic fashion. Ramkrishna Mukherjee conceptualised his methodology by differentiating between the 'inductive-inferential' and 'deductive-positivistic' methods of research. The chapter on Mukherjee argues that his reliance on the inductive-inferential method as better than, what he calls, the deductive-positivistic method lacks any substantive reason, and is self-justificatory. In practice he does not really go into the more intricate, foundational, justificatory and analytical problems of induction and probability. Mukherjee also believes that the inductive-inferential method is somehow free from the positivistic trap, which, in fact, is a mistaken understanding of positivism. Mukherjee's inductive social science shares all the major elements of positivistic thinking that are evident in the methods he rejects. And finally, one of the ironies of Mukherjee's methodological prescriptions is that though he rejects the deductive model as positivistic, inadequate, subjective and value-loaded, he ultimately takes recourse to the deductive reconstruction of his inductive methodology! Thus, in spite of his best efforts and his apparent rejection of the deductive mode of inference, it creeps in stealthily into his framework and takes over his whole scheme – a fatal flaw that virtually demolishes his entire theoretical edifice.

What is interesting in this shift of paradigm from early sociologists to the research agenda of Mukherjee is that 'value' gradually becomes a problematic concept over time. Radhakamal Mukerjee believed that a basic requirement in reordering human society is the recognition of the contribution of values towards the evolution of a new social order. The 'value-free' science, according to him, fails to understand the totality of human life. For Ramkrishna Mukherjee and his contemporaries 'objective' social science requires value-free methods. The quantitative data produced by such 'scientific' methods legitimise the scientific status of sociology and also exclude 'unsystematic' generalities of the tradition of sociology and social philosophy. In the problem of body counts implied by such methodologies, what is not always apparent is that such exercises create not only types and classes but also homogeneous bodies within categories because numbers by nature flatten idiosyncrasies and create boundaries around these homogeneous bodies. In this sense statistics are to bodies and social types what maps are to territories: they flatten and enclose.

André Béteille in a perceptive essay on newness in sociological enquiry wrote:

> The problem with us is not that the small amount of good work done by preceding generations is unjustly criticised by succeeding ones, but that it is ignored and quickly forgotten. In India, each generation of sociologists seems eager to start its work on a clean slate with little or no attention to the work done before. This amnesia about the work of their predecessors is no less distinctive of Indian sociologists than their failure to innovate. (Béteille 1997: 98)

The aim of this book is not simply to narrate the contributions of early sociologists but to criticise and appreciate their intellectual concerns. The purpose of the book is not to write a history of Indian sociology but to raise certain theoretical issues about the historical trajectory of Indian sociology. The theoretical issues raised in this book are to be taken only as initial statements. As the book offers a critical appraisal of Ghurye and Ramkrishna Mukherjee, the essays also highlight the epistemic frameworks of sociologists in the formative years, especially their writings around the concept of man. Writings by sociologists on the ontological and ethical nature of man are not simply a matter of historical curiosity but are both relevant and important for contemporary thought and politics. This book describes a journey of Indian sociology where man eventually disappeared from the theoretical constructs of sociologists. While sociologists have changed their worldview, philosophers have continued to deliberate and reflect on the predicament and destiny of man. Whether man can at all be brought back into sociology and whether Indian sociologists have the energy, imagination and theoretical acumen to undertake this task in future remains to be seen.

ONE

RADHAKAMAL MUKERJEE (1889–1968)
Conceptualising a Cosmological Vision of Man

Critique of Man in Modernity

Radhakamal Mukerjee (1889–1968) was a social scientist of extraordinary talent and scholarship, a social activist, social and economic theorist, creative philosopher, professor at one of the most prestigious universities of his time; he left an indelible mark on multiple fields of social science and irreversibly shaped the course of sociology in India. Though his academic journey began as a theorist of 'Indian' economics, his interest and command over different forms of knowledge naturally pushed him towards an interdisciplinary social science and his writings embody an exceptionally rich range of generalisations, embracing disciplines such as economics, politics, sociology, ecology and social philosophy. He believed that society is not divisible, but that social sciences from analyses and specialisation have fragmented it. In this context let me emphasise that one of the exceptional qualities of the early sociologists of India, that is rarely visible today, was their deep interest in the predicament of man in the era of modernity and their vision to formulate an alternative, holistic conception of man in society. Mukerjee maintained that normal man is a whole person as normal society is an integrated whole, and that it is the task of the social sciences to devise methods to restore both the unity of a human being and the integralness of the social order (Mukerjee 2005b [1960]: 13).

Like Dhurjati Prasad Mukerji, his colleague in Lucknow University, Radhakamal was a critique of man in modern society whom he viewed as fragmented and atomistic. He believed that social philosophy needs to discover society 'which is not a mere aggregate of atomised individuals bound together by the impulses of gregariousness and fear or by rationalism evolved in the reciprocal adjustment and compounding of egoistic interests' (Mukerjee 2005b [1960]: 155). The question of man, which occupies such a central place in Mukerjee's writings, merits our attention not because of its historical significance but more importantly because it is a contemporary issue and many important social philosophers have expressed similar anxiety about the modern individual. Mukerjee has written about the dividedness and hollowness of the individual's life in modern society; he has pointed out that the essential nature of social organisation in modern industrial society has progressively pushed man into a smaller and more specialised involvement in the affairs of the whole community (Mukerjee 2006 [1966]. Atomistic individualism has made man devoid of warm mutuality, community feeling and resulted in the loss of opportunity to bring one's total personality to bear upon the world. He argued that the mechanised relations of specialised functions create a loss of spontaneity and lack of capacity for creative and constructive thought. Mukerjee thought the divisiveness of man is a product of the heterogeneous social sciences, each discipline viewing man in its own separate way. Similarly the unity and wholeness of society, for him, depend on the unity of man. Social reality reflects the experience of man as a house divided against itself.

In the modern era, Michel Foucault believed that the rise of the modern individual and that of the *concept* of society are joint developments, and both developments are what he calls instrument-effects of special historical forms of power.

The modern individual—objectified, analysed and fixed—is a historical achievement. Power and knowledge do not perform their operations on a universal person. Rather, the individual is the effect and object of a certain crossing of power and knowledge, and a product of multiple complex strategic developments in the fields of power and human sciences. Foucault pointed out that the target nowadays is not to discover what we are, but to refuse what we are: the problem of our time is to liberate us from the type of individualisation linked to the state. The task is to promote new forms of subjectivity through the refusal of this kind of individuality which has been imposed on us. Modernity has impoverished the relational world, and it is the duty of man to fight this impoverishment. Foucault wrote: 'Rather than arguing that rights are fundamental and natural to the individual, we should try to imagine and create a new relational right that permits all possible types of relations to exist and not to be prevented, blocked, or annulled by impoverished relational institutions' (Foucault 1997: 158). It is in this context that Foucault talked about 'de-individualisation' (Foucault 2000: 109). In an essay entitled 'The Political Technology of Individuals', Foucault argues that the question 'what is man?' needs to be investigated in terms of further questions like 'what are we in actuality?', 'what are we today?'. 'He proposes that we should open up a new field of historical reflections on ourselves and suggests further questions for investigation: 'There is now another field of questions I would like to study: the way by which, through some political technology of individuals, we have been led to recognise ourselves as a society, as a part of a social entity...' (*ibid.*: 404). He concludes that the emergence of social science cannot be isolated from this political technology, and if man became an object for several different sciences, the reason has to be sought not in an ideology but in the existence of the politics operational in society.

Though Mukerjee does not consider the question of power and political technology shaping the individual, he argues about distortions in political theory which, by exaggerating and compartmentalising the treatment of power, have blocked the development of a 'wide-minded social science theory of equality and freedom, rights and political obligation' (Mukerjee 2005b [1960]: 76). It has to be remembered that Mukerjee is especially interested in the multiple developments of social science that shaped the idea of the modern man. In other words Mukerjee explores the discursive formation of the notion of man and then produces a critique of this idea.

Fragmentation of Man

The roots of Mukerjee's interdisciplinary approach lie in the training he received in English literature, history, and philosophy during his undergraduate studies at the Presidency College in Calcutta under the influence of the nationalist movement following the Partition of Bengal in 1905. Mukerjee was keen to seek answers to the 'grave national issues of Indian misery, exploitation and subjection' (Mukerjee 1997: 66) and he decided to study economics, the subject he thought could provide him the answers. Accordingly he took admission in the combined course of economics and sociology introduced in the university in 1908 at the initiative of its visionary vice-chancellor, Asutosh Mukerjee. Mukerjee obtained his Master's degree in economics and sociology in 1910. He writes, Asutosh Mukerjee 'separated Economics from other branches of knowledge in the M.A. and made specialisation in Economics and Sociology possible in 1908. I belonged to the first group of students to take the M.A. degree in Economics and Sociology under the new regulations of the Calcutta University (*ibid.*: 66–67). Mukerjee's strong opposition to the compartmentalisation and fragmentation of social science, which we will discuss, stems from his early training at the university. Mukerjee writes that what impressed him most in this period by the study of social sciences and social philosophy was the broad humanism of the early social thinking and the universal humanistic ingredients of the 'great founders'. He writes: 'somehow an integrated study of the various social sciences of Economics, Political Science, Social Philosophy and Sociology stimulated in me the desire and striving to envisage man, society and civilization as wholes that defeat any compartmentalization and its aims' (Mukerjee 1997: 68).

Mukerjee asserts that man is the same everywhere, seeking different values in different social contexts; however the segregation of different aspects of life has brought about the crisis in man. He writes: 'Man is today divided in his mind, loyalties and ways of living because Psychology, Economics, Sociology, Political Science, Law, Ethics and Religion, all interpret human motives and actions in different ways and refuse to see man, society and the way of human living as integrated wholes' (Mukerjee 2005b [1960]: 11). He argues that economics and politics, for example, attempt to treat man only as subjects driven by the quest for wealth and power, while disciplines like ethics, philosophy and religion discuss ideals of goodness, justice, etc., completely ignoring man's relation to fellow men in the economic and political sphere. He regrets that sociology, denying the integrative and comprehensive theoretical pattern of its origin, has also fallen victim to the reigning tendencies of abstraction, isolation and specialisation. He blames the dominant individualism, utilitarianism and 'scientism' of the age that have distorted the original aim of a philosophical integration of all knowledges in sociology.

The artificial division of man in terms of heterogeneous disciplinary discourses, according to Mukerjee, produces a notion of an abstract individual that undermines the social-self integrated into a network of relations. Mukerjee writes that a false metaphysical individualism has constituted the basis of inadequate or false theories and concepts in social sciences:

> In economic theory the unit of treatment is the individual who is isolated from his social and institutional milieu, motivated by single economic drives, and feverishly engaged in production of "goods" that bears little relation to the human values or moral aspirations of life ... that alone make society possible. ... In political theory individual is again pictured as the centre of power, wresting certain abstract, unconditional and costless "rights of man" from the state that becomes the focus of class struggles for dominance both in reality and in theory.... Sociological theory similarly emphasises the elemental instincts and

> drives of the individuals ... that lowers his moral and intellectual level making him irrational, impulsive and anti-social. (Mukerjee 2005b [1960]: 77–78)

Mukerjee on the other hand believed that the imperative need of the social sciences is to replace the concept of the abstract individual by that of the person integrated into a network of values that comprise the ground of all value experience in social life.

For Mukerjee the philosophy of social sciences has to recognise the dialectical nature of man's being and becoming, his reality and appearance, and should be able to understand man's endless quest for the whole. The dialectic is reflected as man's struggle with the dual nature of the self and the ability to measure the reality of the self and society. For example, man's relation with the neighbour becomes at the same time a relation with the self; the neighbour, contrary to common-sense belief, neither warps nor limits man's self-actualisation but helps man in true realisation of the self: 'He who loves his neighbour can alone fully understand and realise himself. Social values and ideals become his own potentialities; social status becomes self-status or self-esteem. He becomes a society, the unending ideal communion of the universe, in himself; he elevates social relationship into a full experience of transcendence, and goals and values into cosmical aspirations' (Mukerjee 2005b [1960]: 5).

Mukerjee considered value as one of most important constituents of social life. He was, therefore, critical of sociology as a discipline basing itself on the abstract concept of the individual like other social sciences, eschewing value consideration. He thought this was a faulty methodology which introduced a certain matter-of-factness to human goals and values and treated them as largely immoral. This was, for him, a pragmatic-positive approach to the study of social relations based on the existing status-power system. The exclusion of values in social analysis became a serious ideological obstacle to the development of, what he called, normal and wholesome human social life, relations and values. As a result, individuals find themselves confused and divided in their mind, and this antithesis between moral man and immoral society becomes the root cause of social frustration and aggression in modern culture. Mukerjee believed that normal man is a whole person just as normal society is an integrated whole.

Man and Value System

Mukerjee views society not as some kind of super-imposition demanding rigid conformity from social beings; rather society, for him, is a mirror of man's desires, values and aspirations. He considers man-value-culture as a restless whole contrary to the nineteenth century evolutionary sociology which viewed them in terms of reciprocal adjustment and conformity. For him value dimension is extremely important for sociology because the central concepts of social science, according to him, are freedom and realisation of human potentialities rather than adaptation and adjustment. He defines human values as long-term goals that have emerged in man's evolution and directed and regulated human behaviour adaptation (Mukerjee 2005c [1964]: 16–17). He considers awareness, utilisation and transmission of values uniquely human, and that man has the capacity to expand the range of values. He writes:

> With the aid of values man delays his satisfactions and fixes his mind and behaviour to distant and sometimes unrealizable goals, strivings and ideals. His value-judgement enables him to choose between alternative courses of behaviour, and solve chronic inner tensions and conflicts by accepting standards and demands that control him from beyond. (*ibid.*: 17)

Mukerjee claims that the system of values has enabled men to direct their development and progress according to their own conceptions of 'all-round freedom, wholeness and transcendence that [their] intelligence, imagination and intuition freely and freshly reveal' (*ibid.*).

He argues that human values emerge due to two factors: first due to the influence of society, its meanings and norms on the individual's needs; second, the individual's own awareness, choice and judgement in need fulfilment. These are interdependent processes. He considers values as essentially social products, but at the same time values include the individual's own assumption of certain goals and purposes. Man is a resident of two domains: the domain of actualities and the domain of values and possibilities. Mukerjee believes that man, thus split into subject and object—that is, man as a striving, evaluating and transcending self and man as a part of the given, conditional, objective world—has the ability to resolve this split into the unity of being. He writes: 'Values, then, comprise a facet of transcendence. The ground of values is man's authentic or essential being wherein is resolved the basic dichotomy or cleavage between subject and object, self and world, egoism and altruism in human experience' (Mukerjee 2005c [1964]: 84). The self can thus extend and transcend without limit and thereby possess the totality of values of self, other and cosmos. The being is thus harmonised and unified with the fusion of truth, harmony and goodness. Thus values as stable, standardised and hierarchical goals in human living transform from life-maintenance through social integration to self-transcendence.

Mukerjee maintains that in the Western philosophical tradition values function as a mode of self-actualisation, whereas in the Eastern social philosophy the concept of value begins and ends with the cosmos; the normal person, in other words, is cosmically oriented. At the top of the human value hierarchy are values that are concerned with transactions with the cosmic and the transcendent. In abolishing the self in neighbour, mankind and cosmos, men realise and fulfil their true nature. Human personality is thus capable of extending itself through self-actualisation and self-transcendence, human goals and values are accordingly related to the whole, the cosmic and the transcendent. Mukerjee criticises phenomenalism because he believes that this philosophy has reduced man's status to a crowd or mass-man and robot with no private self, conscience or intention. On the other hand, modern existentialism, he writes, has found man alone, abandoned and helpless, living in 'bad faith'; the individual subject is trapped in a form of self-deception and unable to grasp the truth of the situation. Contrary to such social philosophies, Mukerjee believes: 'Human person finds the fulfilment of his values and possibilities through the ever-changing, ever-expanding "transaction" between his inner life and outer cosmos. The more he transforms himself from a microcosm to macrocosm in essential respects, the more does he actualise his higher transcendent nature' (2005c [1964]: 125). Mukerjee calls this a process of 'cosmocisation' which, he thinks, is necessary for the wholesome and 'homeostatic' living of man and also for his or her survival and advancement as a species. The process, according to him, yields the cosmic person and unlimited society of the cosmos as the final products of evolution. The transactions between the cosmos as a whole and the personal cosmos, that is, the community of other persons, undergo continual transformations. For Mukerjee, then, the triad pattern of person-values-cosmos is crucial because there is a striving in them for an ideal wholeness, coordination and synthesis exhibiting the essential unification of being and cosmos. Man's comprehension and appreciation of the unity of life and things reshape persons-values-cosmos in their reciprocal interdependence and continuity. Mukerjee quotes Heidegger to the effect: 'The question of man is not an anthropological question, but a historically metaphysical question' (*ibid.*: 126).

The four fundamental principles of cosmic evolution according to Mukerjee are: individuality, openness, integration and transcendence. These principles become the values, norms and purpose of human living and are linked with human fulfilment and perfection. He asserts that the concept of man as the creator of open, whole and transcendent values can alone bring social-humanistic and philosophical theories of values under a common denominator. He claims that without man, the cosmos becomes trivial and irrelevant, but at the same time, intercommunication between the cosmos and man make human beings the focus of a value system. His fundamental thesis is that social beings cannot live in ego-centric isolation, nor can their desires be fulfilled in such manner; they can only be realised through social intercourse and cooperative actions and like tools and language, man's values are a means of directing social interaction. Thus values emerge as a result of the fulfilment of urges of individuals in contact with other individuals in society (Mukerjee 2005a [1949]: 68–69). The concrete world in which man lives is a world of particulars, contingencies, imperfections, values of unique individuals; however, the real being belongs to the unity of the whole and is thus immanent. For Mukerjee, no value theory can be adequate unless it combines the universal with the particular, the transcendent with the immanent, the complete with the incomplete values and value experiences. The notion of the immanence of transcendent values as universals of the moral life of individuals enables them to fulfil their possibilities, advance beyond their finite existence and become participants in the universality of the cosmos. Mukerjee claims that man is a split being and lives simultaneously in different orders or dimensions of value experience. Man is a living nexus of complementary values of transcendence and immanence. However all antinomies of values and realities, existence and essence are harmonised and synthesised in the transcendent, ontological unity of being.

Communitarian Man

In his book *The Dimensions of Values: A Unified Theory* (2005c [1964]), Mukerjee stresses the interpersonal nature of human existence and transcendence. As discussed above, he has highlighted the unity, mutual involvement and fusion of all values and possibilities as harmonising principles of life. In his next book *The Community of Communities* (2006 [1966]), he attempts to extend and develop the same ideal of the open human person-in-communion for the understanding and interpretation of human communion and community. Mukerjee asserts that the philosophy of community is based on the open triadic system of human person values and community in their dynamic reciprocity and togetherness. He thereby affirms the potentialities of the human community for passing over to the universal trans-community of communities. The triadic elements, namely, human person, values and community are unities, but they are transcendences as well. For Mukerjee, man's identification with the largest unity, the cosmos, can alone be the basis of a meaningful, forward-oriented notion of mankind. The key ideas to achieve this are open communication, communion and community. Mukerjee believes in the *Upanishadic* idea that 'the cosmos is a single nest for mankind' (2006 [1966]: 8).

Mukerjee argues that in this age of fragmentation and division, man is estranged from his real Being and hence the community he or she experiences appears as coercive or punishing. Mukerjee calls this the perverted form of community which is the 'socially conditioned, packed, drilled, dumb-driven crowd, mass or collective, founded on the impersonalised' (Mukerjee 2006 [1966]: 8). This environment makes men forget their true community, which is based on authentic communion and interfusion of the self and the other. He proclaims that acknowledgement of true community as an ontological notion by the social sciences can alone resolve the moral crisis of the age produced by the polarity between individualism and totalitarianism. He reasons that community is never created through law or force but is born in the minds of men, and it is man's free, transcending self in-and-with community that defines and constitutes personality. He writes: 'Man is most fully transformed into personality by the true community—the community of communities' (2006 [1966]: 9). For him the social crisis of the age can be resolved only by a new ontology of community based on centrality of self-in-communion and the cosmos apprehended by it.

For the enrichment of life, values and community, man continues to expand his or her cosmos and its resources. The philosophy of community conceives it as the pattern of one cosmos, one community. The human self, values and community have the double possibility of making themselves fragmentary, isolated and individualistic or enjoying wholeness, transcendence and communitarian prosperity. This is related to the achievement of unity, fullness and transcendence of self rather than its actuality. Within the limited bounds of a finite environment and society this is the total human achievement of one cosmos, one community. This is a process that ensures unlimited extension of man's single, personalised cosmos, the community of communities, and is organically linked to universality and transcendence of man's self. At the peak of this process man realises the unity and continuity of the self with mankind and cosmos, resulting in the transformation of the finite into a participation in some measure of the cosmic life. Mukerjee believed that human experience is community experience.

Mukerjee argues that in the West the term 'society' is associated with impersonal and pragmatic relations and the term 'community' refers to those associations based on positive relations as bonds. He writes: 'Western political and social theory would largely identify society with the state and attribute its necessary unity to law backed by power or threat of punishment. The modern western concept of the human community is as mechanical as the Cartesian world of discrete, atomic, unrelated human selves' (Mukerjee 2006 [1966]: 17). But Mukerjee argues that man's moral and cultural advancement shows the resourceful, transcending self of man establishing relations with all possible selves. Selfhood is thus an open system of communion with other selves and implies self-actualisation and self-expression through a ceaseless striving after the universal community. Communion involves commitment and responsibility of self for the other in the process of self-actualisation.

The philosophy of community, according to Mukerjee, is founded on a dual perception: first, that the personality, values and community are intricately interconnected in an endless interchange and unity; and second, that each coordinate, namely, person, values and community, unravels unforeseeable and self-transcending potentialities through dynamic, mutual interpenetration. This is because every man is a part of the single unlimited cosmos and is concerned with its forward oriented purpose to ensure the fulfilment of cosmic values. Human possibilities and potentialities can be realised only through this process. What is important is not the egocentric, fragmented man but man in communion or the *Homo universalis,* who is one with the community of mankind and with the moral cosmos of the community of communities. Each man's moral aspiration is to become the whole and complete *Homo universalis.*

The boundary of a community can be enlarged through the progress of communication. As Mukerjee writes: 'Human society in this age enlarges itself into the community of mankind through the improvement of world expression and dissemination of knowledge, world understanding, and world co-operation....Finally communication is a metaphysical category of all possible communities establishing the identity of self with the generalised other, the cosmos' (2006 [1966]: 96). In other words communication at this metaphysical level is the longing and capacity of every man for identity, continuity and wholeness which signals man's kinship with cosmos-total. Thus, for Mukerjee, communication, communion or community march together in the progressive unfolding of man, values and community values, internalised, communicated and transmitted by man are product of communitarian relations. Mukerjee argues that community extends from family, kin-groups, tribe, nation and mankind into the absolute and eternal community of communities.

Mukerjee rejects Bertrand Russell's view that the cosmos is meaningless, purposeless, totally indifferent as to how man lives. He also reflects Søren Kierkegaard's view of man as abandoned by the cosmos, lonely, helpless and full of anguish, and depiction of community as a crowd, untrue, impersonal and bleak. Mukerjee believes man has the capacity to transform the cosmos into an intimate, reciprocating community. He further asserts that man is in the universal community as the universal community is in man. 'The finite and the infinite, the universal and the individual, being and becoming enter into each other. The drop is in the ocean and the ocean is in the drop' (2006 [1966]: 105). The cosmos embodies unrealised values of its own and at the same time has the potentiality to enrich itself by unknown and unpredictable human values.

This particular tendency points to the total fulfilment of values for all to achieve. Each person, as a component of the community of cosmos, thus aids the maximum fulfilment of potentialities for all beings belonging to it.

In this context it is important to understand the way Mukerjee differentiates between communication and communion. Mukerjee writes: 'Communion implies a dynamic interchange between the self and the other in which both actively enter and fuse into each other. Communication, on the contrary, is the way of behaviour adjustment to fellow man and the social world that does not primarily evolve any deep and subtle reciprocal human meaning' (2006 [1966]: 110–111). Interpenetration of minds lies at the root of authentic communion and failure in this reduces communion to the phase of communication. A genuine communion, therefore, yields complete understanding and appreciation of both the self and the other or what Mukerjee calls 'self and cosmos-reality—universal meanings, values and relations' (*ibid.*). In contrast to the depth and profoundness of communion, communication is superficial and thin. According to Mukerjee modern mass media produced by industrial mass culture uses various techniques of communication like advertisement, propaganda to promote an awareness of minds to one another. But he dismisses this form of connection as thin, superficial and unstable communication that cannot be called communion.

Mukerjee states that men cannot annul their finiteness but they can break it. This breakthrough is achieved through man's communion and living in community. It is through this process that 'man becomes a community' and achieves his or her true society in the community of mankind-and-career, namely, person, values and community, interchange through integration, completion and fulfilment of the individual as *Homo universalis* beyond empirical existence. Mukerjee writes:

> Man has essentially a dual nature. He is finite and infinite, particular and universal, actuality and potentiality, appearance and reality. His transcendence is the sure index of his humanness. It is not by his finiteness, form, relation, and existential situation, but by his infiniteness,

> universality and transcendence that he is fully aware of his humanness. The open, whole and transcendent self is the real self man. (Mukerjee 2006 [1966]: 121–22)

Transcendence and Self-actualisation

Two key-concepts that Mukerjee deploys in his theory of the cosmological conception of man are transcendence and self-actualisation. The troubles of a calamitous twentieth century are aggravated and tend to become unmanageable as men are caught up in divisive forces that divide the personality of modern man. They lack the type of social relationship that gives them a deep appreciative understanding of both their fellows and themselves. Mukerjee believes that man lives an immediate, irrational existence but at the same time restlessly seeks meaningful harmony and solidarity of living in a universal whole. In other words men behave as gross physical beings, but they also identify themselves with some 'essence', 'harmony' or ordained pattern. Thus they go beyond themselves and society towards unity and wholeness. Men find their true selves and true society through a constant dialectic between their irrational immediate selves and their essential, indeterminate selves. Men are capable of transforming their finite individuality into the seat of the infinite. Mukerjee calls this the trans-human, trans-social urge of man and considers this tendency as an essential element in man's self-becoming. He argues that man is real only in so far as he or she is part of the universal, unlimited society. Man's self-actualisation and transcendence are essential for the creation of the 'real' man. Thus man's behaviour is essentially qualitative and dynamic, rising from level to level.

Mukerjee believes that human personality is always 'open' and this openness is rooted in man's basic capacity for self-transcendence. The open personality strives for wholeness, harmony and transcendence. The open personality abhors closeness, separateness and fragmentation and endeavours to build up a universal and harmonious community of mankind. The philosophy of man, according to Mukerjee, is grounded in the conceptualisation of man's 'self-actualisation' and 'self-transcendence'. Through these dual modes of fulfilment the human personality transforms itself and the other. From the viewpoint of the philosophy of mankind, man must be considered as a person in a community of persons. Mukherjee writes: 'The two basic psychological processes of human development, self-actualisation and self-transcendence and the two metaphysical categories of being and becoming, immanence and transcendence, are correlated to each other in the dynamics of human personality' (2005d [1965]: 88). It is thus human personality that progressively seeks openness, universality and transcendence, and human community ever enlarges its boundaries and embraces mankind-as-a-whole.

Mukerjee considers affiliation, extension and transcendence as the core of human growth. These qualities enable man to rise from a given biological situation to the ideal or transcendent dimension. This transcendence characterises man's effort to identify with non-self, abstract mankind and cosmos-reality. Mukerjee believes that man strives for perfection by going beyond selfhood through transcendence. 'Through transcendence man in all epochs and countries transforms the cosmos into an intimate reciprocating community' (2006 [1966]: 106). The transcending self of man far surpasses the boundaries of family, neighbourhood, class, nation and draws man away from his or her individuality towards the 'all-togetherness of the cosmos'. He defines the cosmos in the following manner: 'In which re gathered together all sentient creatures from amoeba to mankind and all insentient things from atom to galaxy....The cosmos is essentially a single order of being—an intercommunicating, interchanging, interacting personal order' (2006 [1966]: 108).

Mukerjee submits that 'mankind-and-cosmos' as a whole is the largest totality which man's transcending mind can contemplate. This approximates to Being or reality. At the deepest level of the human mind mankind and cosmos become identical, all men being part of a single cosmos, a single reality. He believes that without this ontological experience the universalising transcending self cannot achieve inner poise, harmony or the full range of depth of communion and community-cosmos in totality. The universal life of the cosmos as the community of communities is grounded in freedom and wholeness. The individual through this process of transcendence becomes at once the product of, and the participant in, this universal life. This is because self-transcendence generates the sense of the whole and the transcendent and both qualities are mediated by man's community.

Self-hood is moulded by the human community, and the human community on the other hand is rooted in the individual's positive self-identification and empathy which unite them as a group. Mukerjee writes: 'Neither the Hobbesian view of the community based on constraint nor the Lockean or Rousseauian postulation that is based on consent or contract does justice to the communion, interchange and interfusion between self and the other that underlie normal human growth and self-actualization' (2006 [1966]: 18). Mukerjee argues that any theory of man which is specialised, compartmentalised and segmented in a narrow, limited perspective provides a wrong image of man. Such theories discount man's creativity, freedom and his or her striving for harmonious and wholesome relations. The dissociation of social sciences from one another yields a distorted, segmented and archaic picture of man and society. He asserts that there is a need for integral discourses because only an integrated social science can recognise man's striving for unity and wholeness. He asserts that 'man needs the cosmos-as-community in order that he can achieve his wholeness and completeness' (*ibid.*: 137). Mukerjee takes up the issue of both the crisis in social science and the life of modern man in his book *The Oneness of Mankind* (2005d [1965]).

Oneness of Mankind

I have already mentioned that Mukerjee denounced the compartmentalisation of social theory and argued for rethinking the goals of the social sciences in a universal perspective. He attempted to formulate the theory of the oneness of mankind, embodying a new dimension of social analysis. He believed that dissociation of the social sciences from one another produces a distorted picture of man and society. He, therefore, argued for a synthesis of all social knowledge on a global scale. The fragmentation of social science and realities and perspectives of each separate branch of knowledge distorts the cosmos-picture of mankind. He claims that the ideal-system of natural sciences reveals the evolution of cosmos, life and mind in its continuity and togetherness. Social science, in his opinion, should discard the utilitarian and hedonistic view of man's destiny, and only thus can mankind's inherent capacities for global democracy develop.

The philosophy man, for Mukerjee, postulates the open, universal or cosmic mind and the community of mankind-and-cosmos in their togetherness and interpenetration. Mukerjee calls this process the 'cultivation of trans-humanism' which can proceed under the feeling of togetherness for all men everywhere. Such humanistic notions are both *qualitative* and *quantitative*: qualitative in the sense of their spiritual values and experiences of truth, justice, love; quantitative because the human community ever enlarges its boundaries and embraces mankind-as-a-whole. Man advances from one stage of human self-awareness, self-actualisation and self-transcendence to another only in one direction: from fragmentariness to wholeness and universality.

It is in this context that Mukerjee discusses the concept of culture and argues that an authentic interpretation of culture is possible only through an understanding of the dynamic interchange between personality, values and community. Hence, according to Mukerjee, man, values and culture show a total articulation and movement towards wholeness, universality and transcendence. He argues that the trend of all cultures is the growth and maturation of the cosmic personality type or *Homo universalis*. Mukerjee posits a universal and eternal community of cosmos where the essential Being of mankind can be realised. He claims that his views about mankind are different from the Hegelian conception of mankind and world-spirit, which reveal themselves at certain historical moments or stages as climaxes in world history. According to Mukerjee's interpretation we need not wait for the gradual realisation at the right historical situation of the world-spirit because man can achieve wholeness and universality without an experience of the Hegelian grand climax of world history. Mukerjee writes: 'Personality, values and community, individually and in their togetherness, have an essentially open and self-transcending character in human culture that is missed in the Hegelian notion of mankind and world spirit in its quintessence' (2005d [1965]: 93).

Mukerjee considers individualist ideology as valorising the atomistic, fractional person, disregarding the whole and universal person who seeks and establishes ever more expansive communion and solidarity. The individualistic approach confines human interests within a narrow boundary of interest groups or classes and ceases to be forward oriented. Exaggeration of rights and interests in the individualist ideology, according to him, not only denies the modern political trend of world unification but also the central trend of human nature towards transcendence and universalism. The essential function of human experience in the modern epoch, according to Mukerjee, 'is the transformation of disoriented, sick and aggressive individuals into harmonious, creative and whole persons.... A perennial ideal of *Homo universalis* is embodied in the brief ancient formula: the universe is personal, meaningful and purposeful—the single, common nest of mankind (*Visvam ekanirham*)' (2005d [1965]: 93).

To achieve the goal of what Mukerjee calls 'mankind cosmos', perspectives and aims of the entire study of man require changes. Borrowing from the philosopher Alfred Whitehead, he uses the phrase 'the society of societies of societies' for 'mankind cosmos' and argues for a renovated social philosophy that can help evolve a universalist frame. What is needed is a unified science and philosophy of man. Mukerjee writes: 'Man's knowledge of himself and his knowledge of the Cosmos are inseparable' (2005d [1965]: 96), and this combined knowledge reveals to man the ideal of harmony, wholeness and transcendence.

Cosmological Conception

It is possible to argue that Mukerjee's cosmological conception of man is utopian, idealistic and speculative. However, what is evident from his conception of man is his rejection of modern ideology based on the notion of the individual. In his view of man Mukerjee has worked out a critical reading of modernity that compels our attention and warrants discussion. Mukerjee constructs two contrasting ideologies that he believes are differently related to the future of mankind. On the one hand there is an all-embracing-holistic ideology which valorises not only the social whole but envisages man-with-cosmos as a whole. Man, who corresponds to this vision, is viewed as complete, in harmony with the universe and transcendent. Individualistic ideology, on the other hand, valorises the individual—the independent, autonomous and essentially non-social moral being and accordingly disregards the social whole. Individualistic ideology, according to Mukerjee, projects a distorted picture of society as an aggregate of atomised, segmented, fractionalised individuals bound by egoistic interests. The portrayal of the divisiveness of man has enhanced the troubles of contemporary times because men lack the capacity for productive and positive thought; their isolated existence deprives them of social relationships that give them a profound appreciative understanding of their fellows and themselves. Mukerjee argues that the predicament confuses men and they wonder all the time what they ought to do and consequently are incapable of solving the serious problems that follow in the wake of a dynamic industrial society.

It should be noted that defined in this way, as ideologies with mutually contradictory principles, the two are radically incompatible and no compromise is possible between them. It is possible to question the practicability of returning to holism and universalism within the framework of modern societies. The desire for unity and wholeness that Mukerjee visualises can be reintroduced on individualistic foundations only in the form of a determination to put an end to the division or atomisation of society. Since no consensus is possible on this, society may end up becoming a totalitarian regime.

In fact it is possible to argue that all champions of political individualism, for example Rousseau, have also harboured a kind of nostalgia for the unity guaranteed by the holistic conception. The anti-individualistic strain attempted to recover the *universitas*, and this tendency generated a problem of modern philosophy which is how to construct a social order and preserve the possibility of social unity among humanity made up of individual atoms. Mukerjee in his own way attempted the recovery of *Homo universalis* from a different theoretical vantage point as we have discussed. The speculative and idealistic quality of this venture cannot be denied, but Mukerjee's efforts also demonstrate his frustration with the fragmentation and isolation of human beings in modernity. Mukerjee redefined humanism which, according to him, should consist in thinking of subjectivity as transcendence, and of transcendence as communication. In other words, man's humanity consists in the rupture of identity through openness to the otherness that belongs to the 'other person'. This view of man echos Emmanuel Lévinas's philosophy that pronounced the end of 'the subject turned to itself' (Lévinas 1987: 94).

Mukerjee's firm belief and insistence on the intersubjective rootedness of subjectivity remind us of Kant and Fichte's thinking that 'man becomes man only among men', expressing thereby the ideal of a subjectivity incapable of closing-in upon itself. Lévinas also does not cease to stress that real humanism consists of 'the desire for the other' (Lévinas 1987: 94). Mukerjee through his severe critic of man-in-modernity expresses a certain representation of the subject—precisely the one, in fact, in which 'man shuts himself up like a monad' (*ibid.*). As discussed earlier Mukerjee forcefully argues for the self's openness to otherness or exteriority by stressing like Lévinas that 'Everything human is outside' and that 'Everything is outside, or everything in me is open' (*ibid.*: 145).

The cosmological conception of man valorises wholeness, totality and understands the human being as subordinate to the whole. It is possible to criticise cosmological conception as an ideology which engenders human beings' reducibility to the world; cosmological type classifies man merely as a creature in the world together with other beings. In effect, the human is treated merely as an object which also presupposes the reducibility of man. Radhakamal Mukerjee's colleague at Lucknow University, D. P. Mukerji was also a trenchant critic of the idea of the individual and individualistic ideology, and proposed instead the ideal of person or *purusha,* which attempts to understand men in their innerness, their unique and irreducible character. Man is not just a mere 'man' who is reducible to the world, but a person, a subject that transcends his or her corporeality (see Chapter 3). D. P. Mukerji, therefore, stressed the notion of personality in his writings (Mukerji 1924) and affirmed that the concept of person is broader and more comprehensive than the concept of the 'individual'.

For Mukerjee, cosmology entails both the overarching conceptions of the place of human beings in the general scheme of existence and the forces engaged in the constitution and generation of such a scheme. These forces relate to the relationship between human beings with other living and non-living objects; the overall cosmic processes that these beings represent and the resulting consequence for human experience. One familiar way of exploring cosmologies is in the context of religious beliefs and ritual practice, but Mukerjee's approach is secular in nature. The cosmological argument charts out man's creative drive and the way human beings can orient themselves within their environment. The positive aspect of Mukerjee's cosmological conception is that it articulates a particular space-time vision that sees human beings as intimately bound together with cosmic processes. In Mukerjee's cosmology man occupies a central and pivotal position. The cosmos thus constructed implies a totality of phenomena, unification of mankind, and builds up a universal and harmonious community of mankind.

In debates about the development of the modern world, it is repeatedly posited that in the emergence of the scientific attitude certain cosmological barriers to grasping the nature of existential realities were broken. Human beings were no longer the centre of the scheme of things and their existence no longer had a necessary meaning that was pre-ordained.

However, this view assumes that modern science is not itself a type of cosmology. It also ignores the new understanding of the universe and forms of existence within it that are germinal in many cosmologies, even those that on the surface appear anti-scientific. Mukerjee, therefore, argues for a broad frame of reference and a rethinking of the goals of social sciences in a universal perspective. Mukerjee is against the compartmentalisation of disciplines and has emphasised the unity of sciences in his formulation of the theory of oneness of mankind. Thus Mukerjee's sociological enquiry into the cosmological conception of man concentrates on greater possibilities for man as well as the comprehensive expansion of knowledge. For Mukerjee the idea is not a utopian or fanciful vision, but it is the faith of our age.

TWO

GOVIND SADASHIV GHURYE (1893–1984)

Structuring Caste and Indian Social Order

Ghurye and Indian Sociology

It was in the first felicitation volume in honour of G. S. Ghurye that D. P. Mukerji made his now famous statement that while others were 'Sociologists in India', Ghurye was the 'only Indian sociologist' of that time' (Mukerji 1954: 234). Ghurye's research themes, subjects, style of presentation have prompted social scientists to remark that he is an indigenous, independent and original scholar with a firm grounding in Indian tradition. Mandelbaum, paying him a rich tribute, writes: 'One advantage that Professor Ghurye has had in his studies of India is his thorough grounding in the Sanskrit literature and in the high tradition of the civilization' (Mandelbaum 1976: vi). Ghurye is regarded not simply as a scholar with a solid grounding in tradition but a bearer of Indian tradition as well, and to this effect Mandelbaum cites from Ghurye's autobiography: 'My father in the discharge of his duties as the guardian of the local renown of the family for piety, thought of me, the "reincarnation" of his piously religious father, to be the proper member of the family to carry on the traditions' (Ghurye 1973:

8). Dhirendra Narain, while explaining Ghurye's reclusiveness, his indifference towards Western theories, and his descriptive and empirical orientation, writes: 'Deeply rooted in Indian culture, he has not allowed anything to deflect him. Ghurye has chosen to be a recluse in order to preserve his freedom to do what he thinks best' (Narain 1979: 238). Ghurye himself considered the knowledge of Sanskrit to be essential to the study of Indian society. In an interview Ghurye remarked: 'Throughout my life as a sociologist, I have always tried to use my knowledge in Sanskrit literature in all its branches to enlighten the past social history ... I am a firm believer that whoever wants to do sociology of India in particular, must have a thorough grounding in Sanskrit literature' (Pramanick 1982: 26).

The quotations and assessments cited above give a clear indication about the common image of Ghurye among social scientists. How far does this image match with Ghurye's writings? In this essay I have selected one important book by Ghurye, namely, *Caste and Race in India*, for a critical assessment of Ghurye. Originally published in 1932, the book went through several editions, and I have chosen the fifth edition published in 1969, principally because at this time Ghurye was about seventy-six years old, and definitely expressed his most mature thought on the subject (Ghurye 1969 [1932]). This essay attempts to show that Ghurye's narrative of caste is completely subsumed under the hegemonic colonial discourse on caste. Though he does not make any explicitly theoretical statement nor construct a theoretical model of the system, the positions, notions, concepts, figures, signs, signifiers, methods and inclinations that are implied in his narrative are very much within the order set up by colonial knowledge. In short, this particular narrative, and by implication related texts by Ghurye, betrays the commonly accepted notion about him of being 'an Indian sociologist' rooted in Indian culture.

Caste: Narration and Totalisation

For Ghurye, sociology is a total subject. For him, 'history and sociology are almost the same. History puts its emphasis on political history and wars, while a sociologist has his focus on social history. The greatest historian of the English society, G. M. Trevelyan, was a sociologist because he gave us a picture of the British Society' (Pramanick 1982: 26). Ghurye also adds that in India, there is hardly any scope for making a distinction between sociology and social anthropology and that both approaches must be combined into one. Hence for Ghurye social analysis is a comprehensive totalising activity combining history, anthropology, Indology, sociology and related subjects.

In a similar vein Ghurye's narrative of caste is also a totalising activity, following the familiar narrative form of beginning (origin of caste and 'caste through the ages'), middle ('caste during the British rule,' 'caste and politics'), and end ('a casteless society or a plural society?'). In recent times, narrative has come to be acknowledged as, above all, a human-made structure—never as 'natural' or given. Whether it is in historical, fictional or sociological representation, the familiar narrative form of a beginning, middle and end implies a structuring process that imparts meaning as well as order. The notion of its 'end' suggests both teleology and closure and the narrative becomes a mode of 'totalising' representation. Functionally, the term totalising points to the *process* by which the author renders his materials coherent, continuous and unified—even at the risk of doing violence to them.

For Ghurye, history and sociology of caste should be based on an objective and disinterested compilation of 'facts.' Pillai notes that Ghurye's very first book is prefaced with this quote from G. M. Trevelyan: 'Disinterested intellectual curiosity is the life blood of civilization' and he remarks that 'this explains what Ghurye is doing' (Pillai 1976: 40). Though in such accounts the narrativisation of the problem is hidden and 'facts' seem to speak for themselves, the result is to endow the subject with certain meaning. The employment of the subject is always a totalising representation that integrates multiple and scattered 'facts' and 'events' into one unified story.

A different way of looking at this narrative of caste and race could be to highlight the areas in which interpretation enters the domain of the sociological (nature of caste groups, features of the caste system, caste, sub-caste, kin and so on) and historiographic representation (caste through the ages, race and caste), especially in the choice of narrative strategy, explanatory paradigm or ideological encoding. It is through such means that one can show how various interpretative strategies condition any notion of sociology or history as objective representation, which are basically interpretative representations and given meaning by the very discourse of the narrator. The pose of objectivity and disinterestedness that denies the interpretative and implicitly evaluative nature of sociological representation can be shown to be empty postures through a close examination of explanatory paradigms and ideological encoding of the text. And that is what this essay attempts to do. The basic question that this essay raises is: what is the epistemological status of Ghurye's historical and sociological descriptions of caste? Because we know that both in history and society, all past events and all societal activities are potential historical and sociological 'facts,' but ones that become facts are those that are chosen to be narrated. They get meaning, not existence, by their representation in history and sociology.

With more than twenty-six books to his credit, Ghurye was a scholar with wide interests, who devoted his whole life to the study of Indian society, history, culture and social practices. This essay does not attempt to discredit Ghurye's scholarship, but tries to show that he was also bound by the colonial epistemological authority.

Caste and Empiricism

Modern sociology of caste is related to and often identified with the expansion of the field of perception and observation. Beginning from the nineteenth century, the various volumes on castes and tribes and the description of people in census reports based on field investigations, observations and reorganisation of historical accounts paved the way for the systematisation of caste. The 'truth' is often linked to the sovereign power of this empirical gaze that turns an obscure darkness into light.

Ghurye's account of caste in its own way shares this prevalent discourse of caste. Ghurye, in this account, is an empiricist par excellence, and apparently this empiricism is based on the rediscovery of the absolute value of the visible, 'the facts' and on the predetermined rejection of systems and all their chimeras. Hence Ghurye does not attempt a theoretical account of caste nor is he particularly inclined towards this task; he would rather prefer a precise empirical description of caste. It is interesting to note that in many instances in his account of caste, possibilities of making theoretical gestures do arise, but Ghurye carefully avoids them. Narain in his account of Ghurye points out:

> The one abiding lesson he learned at Cambridge and sought to transmit to his students was respect for facts. When he began his career, very little work had been done in sociology in India, and it was salutary to insist on facts.... Ghurye's commitment to facts has both a positive and a negative side. Positively, it has given him and his students a firm empirical base, curbing the speculative tendencies that are especially tempting in the absence of concrete information.... Negatively, Ghurye's prolonged neglect of all theoretical positions, however tentatively, has deprived his writings of a powerful thrust. (Narain 1979: 238)

Being faithful to facts, Ghurye also attempts a faithful description of caste. In fact at the beginning of his book, *Caste and Race in India*, Ghurye points out that a general definition of caste is not available:

> It appears to me that any attempt at definition is bound to fail because of the complexity of the phenomenon. On the other hand, much literature on the subject is marred by lack of precision about the use of the term. Hence I propose to give a description of the factors underlying this system of castes. (Ghurye 1969 [1932]: 1)

Ghurye's indifference to any theoretical positions of the West has been interpreted as his cultural rootedness and creating for him a realm of freedom wherefrom he can devise his own course (Narain 1979: 238). However, as we shall see, Ghurye's description of caste gets itself systematised and organised according to certain procedures which typically characterise the colonial discourse on caste. But before coming to that, let us briefly recapitulate the basic elements of Ghurye's description of caste.

Discourse of Caste

Ghurye's account of caste is characterised by (1) a certain notion of Hinduism; (2) allegiance to racial theory; (3) a search for certain universalistic features of caste in terms of status; (4) an acute focus on the boundary and divisions and subdivisions within caste groups, resulting in the view that subcastes are the 'real' castes; and (5) future direction of castes. For Ghurye the principal features of traditional Hindu society—'when it was ruled by the social philosophy of caste, unaffected by the modern ideas of rights and duties'—can be characterised as follows: (a) segmentation; (b) hierarchy; (c) restrictions on feeding and social intercourse; (d) civil and religious disabilities and privileges of different sections; (e) lack of unrestricted choice of occupation; and (f) restrictions on marriage (Ghurye 1969 [1932]: 2). Operationally, he considers the subcastes as the 'real' castes; he writes: 'There is ample reason why, to get a sociologically correct idea of the institution, we should recognize sub-castes as real castes' (*ibid.*: 20). Ghurye's position was subsequently developed by Irawati Karve in her book *Hindu Society: An Interpretation* and more recently by Morton Klass (Karve 1968; Klass 1980). However, in contrast to Karve and Klass, Ghurye's judgement is purely empirical in nature, or more correctly, Ghurye's view on caste emerges out of his examination of the then available empirical evidences and he restricts himself to this level only without any further theoretical reformulations. This becomes quite evident when we find that Ghurye attempts to explain the difference between castes and subcastes in terms of its empirical functions. He writes: 'Subcastes ... are shown to be real castes by me. However, I have emphasized at the same time the distinct functions of the so-called subcaste and the caste for the individual and the different apperception of them by other groups in the society' (Ghurye 1969 [1932]: 190). I should make myself clear at this point that my aim here is only to show the empirical orientation of Ghurye's writing on caste and not to criticise him for his lack of theoretical acumen.

The third feature of Ghurye's account of caste is based on his understanding of race, which was deeply influenced by Risley, though he differs from Risley in matters of detail. His description of the relationship between race and caste is based on six distinct physical types that he thinks divides the Hindu population. These are: (1) Indo-Aryan; (2) Pre-Dravida; (3) Dravida; (4) the Western; (5) the Munda; and (6) the Mongoloid (*ibid.*: 137). In fact Ghurye's account of the origin of caste is also based on the theory of races and their subsequent admixture at a later stage.

Ghurye also examines the elements of caste and caste-like features outside India. Here he views caste more like a status group and argues that birth and status distinctions are not uncommon in other societies, 'well-marked status-groups within a society, distinguished from one another by rights and disabilities, separated from one another by the absence of freedom of intermarriage, may, therefore, be considered to be a common characteristic of the mental background and social picture of the Indo-European Cultures' (*ibid.*: 159). To this extent Ghurye does not consider caste to be a distinctly Indian phenomenon but would argue that it shares certain common features with status and distinctions found in other societies as well. However, if closely examined, this perspective on caste would tend to contradict the racial view of caste because in the racial view caste would be a unique feature of a particular society associated with its unique racial features.

To sum up, Ghurye's account of caste is based on four different perspectives: (1) Indological views of Hindu society on the basis of which he characterises the main features of Hindu society; (2) racial theory and physical anthropology, on which his account of the origin of castes and the relationship between caste and racial distinctions are based; (3) empirical sociology and anthropology which marks his distinction between caste and subcaste; and finally (4) his account of elements of caste outside India based on orientalist history. It is interesting to observe that the principal sources on which Ghurye depends for his description are the volumes on castes and tribes by Crooke, Risley, Nesfield, O'Malley, Senart, Sherring and the Census Reports. This particular knowledge was produced in the colonial encounter, under the assumption of positivism and the ideology of accumulating factual information, essential racial and cultural distinctions between the East and the West, and the evolutionary or diffusionist theory in social science. Ghurye's approach has been a synthetic one and he adopts the discursive form of the West to describe the institution.

Caste, Race and Colonial Discourse

Now let us examine individually the distinctive features of Ghurye's writing on caste. As I have mentioned, Ghurye's discursive form is not essentially very different from that developed in the West. If we go back in time, James Mill wrote an article on 'Caste' in the 1824 supplement of the *Encyclopaedia Britannica* which was divided roughly into three parts: presumed origin of the system, description of it and criticism of it. Mill presents this institution as having been fairly widespread in antiquity (Egypt, Greece, and Iran). Ghurye, we have seen, follows almost the same model of narration on caste. His account of caste also contains its origin and history, description, caste-like features in other countries and its criticism and future scenario. By this I am not trying to implicate Ghurye of consciously deciding to follow Mill's structure, but on the contrary I am trying to show that Ghurye's discourse on caste follows the established principles and logic of colonial knowledge and that the structure of the discourse had already been set out for Ghurye.

Dumont distinguishes three periods about the main attitudes regarding the history of the Western conception of castes in India. The first period is predominantly explanatory where the caste system is seen to be a shocking or surprising phenomenon and an explanation of its existence is sought. The second period, beginning slightly before this century, is predominantly descriptive in nature, though explanatory tendencies are not altogether absent. Finally, the contemporary period, beginning from 1945, when intensive field investigations began to generate a more precise and detailed description; research into origins is abandoned and replaced by varied sociological considerations (Dumont 1970 [1966]: 22). It must be added that these three periods should not be taken as exclusive but they are overlapping in nature, and each period inherits certain features of the preceding period. Ghurye, obviously falls into the second period, and Dumont is right in his characterisation because along with explanatory sections in the book (especially on the origins of caste, the principal characteristic of the earlier period), description is his predominant concern.

Ghurye's account of the origins of caste is much influenced by nineteenth-century orientalist 'historical' explanations, which were primarily based on three kinds of formulations: the Indo-European or Dravidian theory, the racial theory and the diffusionist theory. Ghurye presents a composite account of caste origins taking his cue from all these orientalist explanations. The Indo-European theory of caste is derived from the presumed entry of a population of Indo-European language and subsequently the theory of caste was provided by Senart in 1896. The racial theory is linked to the Indo-European theory, and derives the institution of castes from the encounter between the two populations: the invaders aiming to preserve the purity of their blood by the creation of a closed group. In fact Ghurye writes:

> It may be taken to be an historical fact that people calling themselves "Arya" poured into India through the north-west somewhere about 2000 B.C. It is equally clear from our discussion that an institution closely akin to caste has been very often described in Sanskrit books, which are the works of either the Aryans or the Aryan-inspired aborigines. Can we trace a close connection between the

> immigration of the Aryans and the rise of the institution of caste? We have seen that the Brahmins, who were the moral guides and legislators of the immigrant Aryans, tried to keep their blood free from any inter-mixture with the lower classes ... Can anthropometry shed any light on this aspect of caste? (Ghurye 1969 [1932]:117–118)

A little while later, after examining the anthropometrical data of Indian people, he concludes:

> In Hindustan ... the gradation of physical types from the Brahmin downwards to Musahar corresponds very closely to the scheme of social precedence prevailing among the Hindustani castes. The state of things can be the result only of such regulations that prevented the possibility of Brahmin blood being mixed with aboriginal blood but allowed the mixture of blood of the other groups in varying proportions. (*ibid.*: 125)

This clearly reflects the nineteenth-century European view of the origin of the caste system, generally expressed in terms of a racial conflict between the fair-skinned invading Indo-Aryan or Aryans and the darker indigenous peoples, the *Dasas* or *Dasyus*. As Cohn writes:

> Nineteenth century European scholars and British administrators attributed their own feelings of racial superiority to the Indo-Aryans, saw them as the bearers of civilization to the Indians, and saw the caste system as the Indo-Aryans' effort to keep themselves aloof and racially pure by relegating the *Dasas* to the lower orders of society and prohibiting marriage with them. (Cohn 1971: 61)

The orientalist reconstruction of Indian society had many facets, a crucial assumption being a fundamental divide between East and West. The orientalist observed the East through Western epistemologies in cognitive relation to the West and initially played a powerful role in the production of official colonial knowledge about India. At a subsequent stage European social theory gained more importance in the production of knowledge, as for instance, evident in census reports and ethnographic accounts, which also shaped Ghurye's account of the caste system. It must be said that the ideology of hierarchy, *Varnashramadharma,* is an important constituent of the ancient knowledge of India, as described in post-*Vedic* Brahminic texts, with its neat ordering of social differences bounded by a moral unity, which continued through medieval *dharmasastra* texts with their more contingent and regionally varied codes. The former received a new kind of legitimacy at the hands of European orientalists, who constructed the knowledge and converted the findings of a valid knowledge and discourse based upon ancient texts into a social theory allegedly pertinent to pre-modern societies of South Asia.

The orientalist construction about Indian culture and society was based on the notion that religion was the guiding principle in this society, the primacy of the Brahmin as the maintainer of the sacred tradition through his control of the knowledge of sacred texts, acceptance of the Brahminical theory of the four *varnas,* and also the general agreement that the practice of Hinduism was filled with 'superstition' and 'abuses.' While the missionaries also accepted this view, the major differences between the orientalists and the missionaries, according to Cohn, 'lay in that the orientalists admired in theory the civilization and religion embodied in the texts and saw the difficulties of Indian society as being a fall from a golden age. The missionaries saw the society and culture as always having been corrupt, pernicious, and filled with absurdities' (Cohn 1990a: 146). So far as caste is concerned, these two viewpoints have been repeated ever since. One view holds that the caste system ideally harmonises the whole with the parts of the system, thereby stabilising and harmonising the social order, while the other would view the system as essentially inegalitarian and corrupting. Ghurye also idealises the past by vigorously pointing out that competition is a modern phenomenon, that 'conflict of claims and opposition has thus replaced the old harmony of demand and acceptance' (Ghurye 1969 [1932]: 301). He laments the fact that 'caste-solidarity has taken the place of village-community' (*ibid.*).

Hinduism and Brahminism

Venugopal, in a perceptive essay on Ghurye, has characterised Ghurye's Hinduism as 'normative Hinduism' and writes:

> His Hinduism revolves around puritanical habits such as abstinence from drink, avoidance of luxuries or epicurean delights, rigorous sexual morals and the pursuit of virtue which are exemplified in the Brahminical way of life. It is significant that he discussed in detail the contributions of Brahmins—who occupied the leadership of Indo-Aryan society—to its making. (Venugopal 1986: 305)

Though as a follower of Rivers, Ghurye, at least theoretically, believed in diffusion and acculturation; however, his works do not imply acculturation as pointed out by Pramanick (1982: 36). While acculturation implies a two-way process or reciprocity, Ghurye in his description of Hinduism describes a process which vertically integrates various groups into a social structure dominated by Indo-Aryanism in general and Brahminical Hinduism in particular. Ghurye locates Hinduism at the hub of this unificatory process, and Brahminical ideas and values form its core elements. For Ghurye, this is the 'cultural unity' integrating various groups, which is being maintained and consolidated in Indian society. This 'cultural unity' is essentially the result of the Brahminic endeavour. As Pramanick points out: 'Thus cultural supremacy of the Indo-Aryans in general and the Brahmins in particular is a matter of unassailable faith for Ghurye' (*ibid.*).

In response to the term 'caste-patriotism' coined by Ghurye to express various caste solidarities, Dumont calls Ghurye's attitude towards caste as his '*Brahminic* patriotism' and points out that 'one comes to assume that if Ghurye deplores caste "patriotism", it is as much out of fondness for an idealized past as out of hostility towards caste; it seems that he believes in the possibility of a transformation which would end caste while preserving *Brahminism* and interdependence' (Dumont 1970 [1966]: 222). Thus Ghurye believes that Brahminism played a decisive role in fashioning Indian social institutions, and that Indian cultural unity is derived from Hinduism. Religion for him is the basis of social unity in India. In this, Ghurye is not much different from orientalists like Alexander Dow (1970), for whom the customs and manners of the Hindus appeared to have largely meant Brahminic prescriptions. In fact the textual nature of the scholarship of the orientalists forced them to accept a particular view of Indian society, namely, that Brahmins as the dominant group in Indian society and located at the centre of the social order, and compelled them to ignore the difference between prescriptive and normative statements derived from the text; nor did they examine the regional variations. Society was viewed as a set of rules which every Hindu followed. This discourse held caste as the foundational core of Indian civilisation. It was caste which held society and its constituent village republics and communities together. It was caste that was responsible for transmission and reproduction of Indian society, and like India itself, caste was seen as based on religious rather than political principles. Oriental essentialising in India regarded caste as the mark of difference from the West, India's essential signifier.

Ghurye follows the same tradition since the book's first publication in the *History of Civilization Series* by C. K. Ogden in 1932. For him also caste becomes the essential signifier of Indian civilisation. It is interesting to observe that Ghurye begins his book from a foreigner's point of view on India. In the very first sentence he writes: 'A foreign visitor to India is struck by the phenomenon known as the caste system' (Ghurye 1969 [1932]: 1). The question at the outset could be: should we then equate Indian society with caste and write the history of Indian civilisation only in terms of caste? Ghurye, however, continues:

> He (the foreigner) may not understand the full working of the system, but he is aware of the fact that Hindu society is divided into groups, known as castes with varying degrees of respectability and circles of social intercourse. This is due not only to the fact that caste is the most general form of social organization in India but also because it presents such a marked contrast to the social grouping prevalent in Europe or America. (Ghurye 1969 [1932]: 1)

Here Ghurye exactly reproduces the argument of 'essential difference' and social *imaginaire* of this supposedly unique Indian institution, valorising the group differences.

Subcaste: Classification and Empiricism

The mode that Ghurye adopts in presenting his narrative of caste is to furnish in his construction a substantial amount of 'factual information' about caste practices, mostly from *Caste and Tribe Reports, Census Reports* and various texts of European scholars. This empiricist orientation of Ghurye grows out of his conviction that 'facts' describe the situation more authentically than any theoretical construction. When asked to comment on the statement that his books are a jungle of facts, Ghurye replied: 'Look, the statement 'jungle of facts' is much preferable to a nicely planned garden of fancies ... and any discriminate reader can turn these facts into fruit bearing garden if he is willing to do so' (Pramanick 1982: 37).

The 'facts' on which Ghurye relies so much for his narrative construction were produced by methods that cannot be said to be specific to India. They were produced under the enlightenment rubric of objective science, what David Ludden (1994) calls 'orientalist empiricism.' The characteristics of the so-called 'objective,' 'scientific' approach merits some attention. The framework is derived from the nineteenth-century intellectual technology developed for the human sciences and consists in the claim of objectivity, of 'value-free scholarship,' which seems to have been more vigorously asserted as a deeper crisis of European culture as it grew. This apparently detached epistemology recognised every new addition to knowledge about India as a new scientific discovery, whose veracity was based on methodologies authorised by scientific standards of the day. Thus this body of knowledge became objectified by the ideology of 'scientific practice,' and in the process projected itself as a set of factualised statements about reality that existed and could be known independent of any subjective, colonising will.

Ghurye's own account of this narrative is that of a 'disinterested (read objective) intellectual curiosity,' a 'scientific and factual' account of the system. In fact, in his autobiography the quotes he uses from the reviews of this book invariably contain the passage that this is a 'scientific study' of caste system in India (Ghurye 1973: 81–86). The factualised representations of India that became official wisdom were conventionalised and then fixed as a factual basis for further inference and theory. The facts were then ordered through classification.

The colonial obsession with the classification of Indian population is well known. The way caste was viewed 'officially' was related to the colonial method of collecting information about the caste system. As Cohn writes:

> In the first instance a caste was a "thing," an entity which was concrete and measurable; above all it had definable characteristics—endogamy, commensality rules, fixed occupation, common ritual practices. These were things which supposedly one could find out by sending assistants into the field with a questionnaire and which could be quantified for reports and surveys; ... This way of thinking about a particular caste was useful to the administrator, because it gave the illusion of knowing the people; he did not have to differentiate too much among individual Indians—a man was a Brahmin, and Brahmin had certain characteristics. (Cohn 1990a: 154)

This was the empirical climate in which information and 'facts' about caste developed into knowledge. There was a new privilege accorded to observation and classifications. As the 'official' census-based perspective of caste viewed the system as one of separate castes and their customs, proper understanding would require classifications to order the data. The new and detailed 'objective,' 'scientific,' classificatory scheme was prompted not simply by the desire of knowledge or for administrative purposes, but also by a search for new ways of connecting things both in the physical world and in the discourse. This was a new way of making history.

Cohn in another essay shows that Indian census, rather than being a passive instrument of data gathering, created by its method, practical logic and form, a new sense of category-identity in India, which in turn created the conditions for reconceptualising group-identities, and had the effect of redirecting important indigenous practices in new directions, by putting different weights and values on existing conceptions of group-identity (Cohn 1990b: 224–254). Ghurye was not unaware of this problem. In fact he saw census itself as having effects on the caste system:

> The conclusion is unavoidable that intellectual curiosity of some of the early officials is mostly responsible for the treatment of caste given to it in the census, which has become progressively elaborate in each successive census since 1872. The total result has been a livening up of the caste-spirit. (Ghurye 1969 [1932]: 279)

However, Ghurye did not question the epistemological authority of this body of knowledge as is evident from the frequent use he made of such information in his book.

When Ghurye insists that subcastes should be recognised as real castes (*ibid.*: 20), he, in fact, carries forward the classificatory method a little further. One of the problems that classification faces is at what stage one should put a stop to it, because classification can proceed indefinitely depending upon the criteria one selects. As we have mentioned, classification is supposed to provide knowledge of empirical individuals on the basis of general characterisation and the method, because it proceeds from identities and differences of the most general kind to those that are less so, and is capable of bringing out vertical relations of subordination. If the system is viewed as a network of interdependence, as Ghurye does, it is important to know what should be the general characteristics, and what order derives the particular features. The system of classification and method adopted by both European scholars as well as Ghurye, rest upon the same epistemological foundation, that a knowledge of empirical individuals can be acquired only from the continuous, ordered and universal tabulation of all possible differences. Method and system are simply two ways of defining identities by means of the general grid of differences.

Looking at the divisions and sub-divisions, it was Senart (1930 [1896]) who first suggested that the subcaste be considered the 'real' group. Senart's concern was to start with a precise idea of the modern state of affairs, and he realised that it was subcaste, the endogamous unit and instrument of internal justice, which was the fundamental institution and which should be called the true caste. Ghurye follows Senart when he points out that subcastes should be recognised as real castes. The main difference between Ghurye and Karve was that Karve believed that castes result from the aggregation of subcastes while for Ghurye subcastes result from the sub-division of castes. This in fact is the difference of inductive and deductive argument or classification of two different orders, one from top down, the other from bottom up. However, in both the cases the search is for a sort of *social substance* existing independently of the system, a substance which will be able to *designate* a group and assist in *derivation* of other features. To conclude, Ghurye's focus on subcaste emerges from his faith in the empiricist social science and his adoption of classification, a passion of the colonial knowledge, and utilising it towards further divisions and sub-divisions.

Caste: Inside and Outside

When Ghurye examines caste-like features outside India in his chapter on 'elements of caste outside India', it appears that here Ghurye is going against the basic grain of colonial understanding on caste, namely that it is this specific institution which centrally and essentially characterises Indian society as radically different from Western society. In fact this was one of the crucial arguments about colonial *difference*. When Ghurye searches for elements of caste outside India, *prima facie* one can argue that Ghurye is negating the argument of colonial difference. But for Ghurye this is the consistent implication if his explanation about racial theory is to be accepted.

Ghurye believed that Indo-Aryans, who established the Brahminic variety of civilisation in this part, belonged to the wider racial group known as Indo-Europeans or Indo-Germans. The Celts, Anglo-Saxons, Teutons, Romans, Spanish, Portuguese and Iranians also belonged to this stock. Because of this common ancestry, 'their separate language diverged yet retained sufficient common structure and content to enable the nineteenth and twentieth-century philologists to group them together' (Ghurye 1969 [1932]: 163). Ghurye's chapter on elements of caste outside India is written to establish this argument. As Pramanick rightly notes that in this section Ghurye attempts to analyse:

> The structural and cultural affinities of the Indo-Aryans with other branches of Indo-Europeans, particularly, with the Anglo-Saxons. He shows that, in respect of caste, the division of labour into caste-like groups is a fairly common attribute of all the branches of the Indo-European peoples, though the peculiar condition of India gave birth to caste in its present form. (Pramanick 1982: 34)

Because of this common trait, the caste-like features can be seen in the endogamous character of the Anglo-Saxon class organisation: 'the law of the Anglo-Saxons laid it down that none was to seek in marriage a mate outside one's class' (Ghurye 1969 [1932]: 157–158). Even in the case of the Indian joint-family, language and religion, cultural affinity is quite evident according to Ghurye. In other words, Ghurye's exploration towards caste-like features in other regions is caused by his search for a common origin and to substantiate his original hypothesis that everything began with Indo-Europeans and Indo-Aryans. Through this search Ghurye is trying to recover the origin, the great source which eventually diversified into so many systems.

Sociology of Caste: Codes of Knowledge

Ghurye's narration ends with a somewhat bleak forecast of coalitions of castes which could occur through the gradual breakdown of rules of exogamy between castes of neighbouring rank, resulting in fragmentation and factionalism through multi-caste and multi-factional alignments. As we have already mentioned Ghurye deplores this possible scenario because of his fondness for an idealised past, fondness for Brahminism which he would like to preserve.

However, in his representation of the past, present or future, Ghurye's narrative is encoded with ideological underpinnings of colonial knowledge. His narration completely accepts the epistemological authority of the orientalist and colonial discourse. As we have seen his understanding of caste in terms of racial theory, in terms of divisions and sub-divisions, in terms of broad features of Hinduism, lacks any indigenous perspective towards this subject. It is as if the basic rules of his narration are already set; Ghurye only fills the relevant gaps.

In other words, the figures of knowledge and those of language, theory and concepts in this narration obey a structure which underlies theories, discourse and sensibility of the times which Ghurye was unable to transgress. In this chapter our intention was to investigate structural 'codes of knowledge' that appear in Ghurye's narration of caste and race, and its own systematic order. We thought that Ghurye's narration of caste and race can be made intelligible in a different way, namely, by showing that they have a systematic structure and theoretical underpinnings, though on the surface the account appears merely a descriptive one. The aim of inquiry was to discover on what basis this knowledge became possible and within what space of order this knowledge was constituted. The discursive strategy that Ghurye adopts in his narration of caste is a result of a generally accepted 'scientific paradigm' of the human sciences that the colonial knowledge propagated. From Ghurye's narrative we have attempted to discover the principal signposts of this derivative knowledge, attempted to show that pure description is not possible, and that there can be interpretations possible in the choice of descriptive categories.

THREE

DHURJATI PRASAD MUKERJI (1894–1961)

Overcoming Individualism: Constituting Man as Person

Introduction

This chapter explores the concerns of D. P. Mukerji on the question of the modern individual and the way he tried to argue for an alternative image, for a different conception of man from the idea of the individual. The man projected by Mukerji is not an abstract, isolated, 'dehumanised' individual, but a being who acquires personality in the society of men. Personality thus attains a crucial theoretical significance in the sociology of D. P. Mukerji. In the present chapter we discuss how in the writings of Mukerji, man constitutes himself or herself as the *person* and moves towards self-transformation. Mukerji believed that the 'gears of modern system' have transformed men as individuals into cogs in the wheels that guarantee society's functioning. In his critique of man's disintegrated existence and tendency to limit man to a function, Mukerji affirmed a revalorisation of the 'person'.

This analysis is not historical sociology in the conventional sense but attempts to trace the pattern of intellectual descent backwards from the present, and in that sense the approach is genealogical in nature. That is why very early in this chapter I have discussed the modern conception and critique of the individual and attempted to move backwards through the sociology of Mukerji. The questions that I seek to ask through this exercise are: what is the nature of our time, what is our 'political ontology', and what are the logics of power that have produced this condition and within which we operate? The answers that Mukerji provides are extremely important in this connection, and it is in this sense that he is our contemporary and it is in this sense that this analysis is not historical sociology. Finally, to grasp the full import of Mukerji's theoretical contributions it is necessary to understand the epistemic matrix of his time. The following section provides a brief account of the sociologists before and after him reflecting on the issue of man and society. It will be evident that Mukerji to a great extent shared the views of the sociologists I have discussed; he also moved the thinking forward by his own original contributions.

Early Critiques of the Individual in Indian Sociology

Before Indian sociology took a narrow empiricist turn, the discourse on society by the early sociologists in India embraced the larger issues concerning man in society. This is particularly evident in their critique of the idea of the individual, which they thought represents an abstract, asocial and dehumanised conception of man. Early Indian sociologists almost without exception were critical of the idea of the individual and individualism. This was both a normative and epistemic position on their part and they all thought the idea of the individual represents a truncated, limited, incomplete conception of man. As Singh (1983: 152) has rightly observed:

> The meta-concepts such as "individual", "person", ... etc. are not merely abstractions of a societal phenomenon but also form its substantive reality: Indian sociologists have long argued that many of the meta-concepts of social

> sciences derived from the West do not have relevance for the Indian society since these are abstractions from a different culture. (Singh 1993: 152)

To provide a few illustrations we can begin from one of the earliest writers of social science in India, Bhudeb Mukhopadhay (1827–1894), who in his pioneering book *Samajik Prabandha* ('Social Essays', 1981 [1892]) objected to the idea of individualism on the ground that it will weaken the social cohesiveness of Indian society. He wrote: 'The force which makes all the families in a society compassionate and somewhat similar to each other is called sociality. And the force which influences each family to be concerned with its own happiness, misery and wellbeing, duties and thereby to live separately, is called individualism' (Mukhopadhyay 1981 [1892]: 94). Bhudeb made no secret of his disapproval of the idea of individualism and considered it harmful for Indian society. He, however, raised a pertinent point when he argued that that in India the colonial regime possessed all the powers, and in such a regime how could it be possible for an Indian to develop individualism.

Radhakamal Mukerjee (1889–1968) criticised the concept of the abstract individual and argued for the idea of *social person*. He thought false metaphysical individualism was the basis of false theories and concepts in social sciences. In economic theory, according to him, the individual was conceived as isolated from his social and institutional milieu, motivated by single atomic drives; in political theory the individual was pictured as the centre of power, having only a certain abstract 'right'. And he wrote:

> Sociological theory similarly emphasises the elemental instincts and drives of the individual or the psychosis of crowds and masses that lowers his moral and intellectual level making him irrational, impulsive and anti-social. It underrates the function of reason in society as arousing and disseminating the meaningfulness and values of community life. (Mukerjee 2005b [1960]: 78)

He, therefore, insisted on replacing the concept of the abstract individual by that of a social self or person who is integrated into a network of institutional relations and values. Mukerjee believed that these relations and values comprise meaning and experience in social life. This point of view opposes the abstracted view of man and argues for considering man as a social being; it considers each man no longer as a particular incarnation of abstract humanity, but as a ground of emergence of a particular collective humanity, of a *society*.

A. K. Saran, who wrote after Mukerji, also shared a similar epistemic framework. Saran, in a complex argument, argues that the misery and the tendency towards self-annihilation of modern man are paradoxically rooted in the grand ideas of man, who has choices, and chooses to live under the threat of nuclear holocaust. He observes that man is in the deepest misery today, and at the root of this despairing situation lies 'the self-grounding, the *causa sui* (or the Man Makes Himself) project of modern man' (Saran 1997: 55). This is the modern conception of the individual, who is self-reliant, self-governed, self-supporting, and has unlimited potentiality for improvement and development. Saran argues that this self-grounding project is based on the postulate of unmediated or self-mediated universal knowability. Self-mediated know-ability refers to the faith that everything in the universe can be fully known, and that man has the required equipment for achieving this universal knowledge. For Saran, modernity is not a particular stage in history, but like Foucault he believes modernity relates to a certain conception of man. In this case Saran argues that the postulate of unmediated universal knowability is the constitutive definition of modernity. Obviously Saran was dissatisfied and frustrated with this paradigm of the modern individual, which he thought was the cause of the present crisis. He believed that the conception of the individual completely forsakes the question of the limits of human knowledge and action. He says traditionally the most important question was what man *ought* to know, for he could then know what he ought to do and what he ought to hope. Thus the question of ethics of man is integrated to the critique of the individualistic notions of man. We will see that this question recurs in the writings of D. P. Mukerji and this combination of sociology and ethics of man represents contemporary thinking on the subject. A more stringent critique of the individual appears in the writings of D. P. Mukerji, as we shall discuss in detail below, who proposed the holistic idea of *purusha* in contrast to the abstracted idea of the individual. According to Mukerji it is the *purusha* which possesses the personality and not the individual. In his Bengali book *Byaktabya* ('Utterance', 1957: 17), he wrote: 'Man will be *purusha,* he will not be an individual, he will be a person'.

The idea of the individual and individualism is generally viewed as key to the understanding of modernity, and those who oppose the idea are considered as backward-looking traditionalists. The critique of individualism by early sociologists is also easily contrasted and explained in terms of divisions like totality/individuality, holism/individualism, society/individual etc. However, in this chapter, I will argue that this critique reflects a deeper anxiety about the way modern power transforms individuals into subjects. In sociology the rise of the modern individual and that of the concept of society (as understood in the social sciences) are joint developments. This particular truth was not unknown to early sociologists. The critique they are producing does *not* tell the story in which the emergence of a science of society announces the increasing autonomy of the individual and the objectivity of the social. Interrogating the conceptual structure of the individual was in a way questioning the protocols of modernity. We find in the writings of D. P. Mukerji concern and disquiet about the society and the knowledges conceived in terms of the individual. But before discussing in detail Mukerji's views let us recapitulate briefly the standard view of the individual and individualism.

The Individual and Individualism in Modern Times

As I have mentioned before, Mukerji's critique of the individual has a contemporary signification. Mukerji thought individualism had a bleak prospect for the future of mankind as many contemporary thinkers. To briefly recapitulate the discourse of the individual and individualism, let me mention that it was Hobbes who first systematically assimilated the idea of the individual in his political theory. His men are for the purposes of his theory identical, equal units. Because they are identical their relations with one another are purely external. Their natures are not affected by the social relations into which they enter. This is the characteristic doctrine of what may be called scientific individualism. It persists in Locke, abandoned by Rousseau and revived again in Bentham. Social and political relations are merely means by which the individual obtains more efficiently what he desired before he entered into these relations. It is possible that the means may be incompatible with the ends for which they are advocated. Since Hobbes' men know no natural restraint of their selfish nature, a despotic authority of the state is proposed. Complete liberty thus has a way of turning into complete absolutism. But politics and social relations do not bite into the nature of individuals. The individuals remain the same unchanged, spiritually isolated atoms.

It is often argued that doctrines of individualism are associated with the rise of capitalism in the West in as much that capitalism required people to be constructed as autonomous and enterprising economic agents, able to relate to one another in a free market. In Marxian thinking the bourgeois mode of production required that men should be free to buy and sell both labour and means of production. In order to argue that an individual could sell labour to others, the physical and mental capacities and activities, of which human labour ultimately consists, must be considered alienable and therefore not an integral or inseparable part of the individual. Since almost everything about an individual was considered alienable—skills, capacities and activities—the crucial question arose as to what was to be considered *essential*, such that its alienation was the individual's alienation and his loss of control over it amounted to his loss of freedom. Bourgeois society by and large located his essential humanity in the interrelated capacities of choice and will. The individual was above all an agent; his actions were uniquely his and therefore his sole responsibility. As long as he was able to choose, his choices were his responsibility. The individual was abstracted from his social background, which could not be considered a co-agent of, and co-responsible for his actions. The individual stood utterly alone, stripped of all social relations, facing the world in sovereign isolation and exercising his conditioned freedom of choice and will. Thus the individual was equated with an abstract mental capacity, namely the capacity to choose and to will, and defined in terms of asocial and 'idealist' concepts. The fact that the concepts of will and choice should have acquired such unprecedented importance in the thought of Hobbes, Locke, Rousseau, Bentham, Kant, J. S. Mill and others should not surprise us.

Individualism pertains to a particular historico-conceptualisation of the person or self. Included within this conceptualisation would be the person's autonomy, self-knowledge, right to privacy, self-sovereignty and self-development. The primary meaning of the word then is of a state or attitude of mind which is naturally produced in a certain kind of society. It is not a society which leaves little scope for individual initiative, but more positively an individualistic society where people 'think for themselves' and are regarded as being 'the best judges of their own interests'. Modern individualism is based on two things: supreme worth of the individual, and the emergence of an economic system dominated by exchange. This individual is quasi-sacred, absolute; there is nothing over and above his or her legitimate demands; his/her rights are limited only by identical rights of other individuals. S/he is a monad in short, and every human group is made up of such monads.

In recent times Foucault demonstrated that power constitutes the very individuals upon whom it operates:

> The individual is not to be conceived as a sort of elementary nucleus, a primitive atom, a multiple and inert material on which power comes to fasten or against which it happens to strike. ... In fact, it is already one of the prime effects of power that certain bodies, certain gestures, certain discourses, certain desires, come to be

> identified and constituted as individuals. (Foucault 1972: 99)

In effect he has described a form of domination that operates by categorising individuals to their identities, a form of power that locates the truth of the individual in his or her sexuality. Conceiving the identity as a fixed and unified entity, post-Renaissance political and post-Machiavellian rationality in the West was concerned with the state as an end-in-itself; the individual was of interest exactly insofar as s/he could contribute to the state. The lives, deaths, activities, work, miseries and joys of individuals were important to the extent that these everyday concerns became politically useful. The emergence of the modern individual as an object of political and scientific concern and the ramifications of this for social life has been a major concern for political thinkers, and Foucault is most important among them.

In Foucault the account that is presented is *not* the triumphant scientific one of Durkheim, in which the emergence of a science of society announces the increasing autonomy of the individual and the objectivity of the social. It is rather the other way round. Foucault tells of the emergence of an objective science of society—one which treats social facts as things—and of the 'mute solidity' of the modern individual in order to show that both are, what he calls, instrument-effects of specific historical forms of power. Foucault wrote:

> This form of power applies itself to immediate everyday life which categorises the individual, marks him by his own individuality, attaches him to his own identity, imposes a law of truth on him which he must recognise and which others have to recognise in him. It is a form of power which makes individuals subjects. There are two meanings of the word subject: subject to someone else by control and dependence, and tied to his own identity by a conscience or self-knowledge. (Foucault 1982: 212)

It is in this context he characterises the modern state as a very sophisticated structure into which individuals can be integrated, under one condition, that this individuality would be shaped in a new form and submitted to a set of very specific patterns. Foucault, therefore, concludes that the ethical, social, philosophical problem of our time is not simply to try and liberate the individual from the state, but also from the type of individualisation which is linked to the state. He asserts that the struggle should not be exactly for or against the 'individual', but against the 'government of individualisation' (*ibid.*: 211). The critique should promote new forms of subjectivity through the refusal of this kind of individuality that has been imposed on us.

D. P. Mukerji's Early Critique

D. P. Mukerji speaks of a new kind subjectivity, rejecting the ideal of the individual, which he thought represents an impoverished relational world. He opposed this impoverished relational fabric in terms of a new subjectivity that he called 'personality'. He wrote about personality in his first book *Personality and the Social Sciences* (Mukerji 2004a [1924]) and he considered this book as a 'personal document ... written with the sole purpose of clearing my attitude towards [a] systematised knowledge of society and life in general' (*ibid.*: vii). He aimed for a holistic conception of man and thought that the abstract individual was too narrow an idea to capture the full essence of man. For Mukerji, the individual was only the starting point of the life process, but life did not stop there. He did not deny that the contemporary social system attempts to make one individual like another; but he also insisted on the life process that moulds and patterns the individual in a variety of ways. He wrote: 'This synthesis of the double process of individuality and the socialisation of the uniqueness of individual life, this perfect unity, I have called Personality' (Mukerji 2004a [1924]: ix). He believed it was a mistake to make the abstract and static individual the pivot of social science theorising, and that mistake needs to be corrected and the concept of personality instead should be made the true pivot.

Mukerji was very much influenced by Rabindranath Tagore's views on personality that Tagore elaborated in his book *Personality* (1917). In his Bengali book *Chintayasi* ('Reflect!',

1933) Mukerji points out his indebtedness to Tagore in thinking of personality as a creative unity. He said it was Tagore who showed in *Personality* how the individual in a creative process loses his/her specificity, establishes multiple relationships and thereby attains unity and universality (Tagore 1917: 72).

Quoting Walt Whitman's poem, Tagore in *Personality* points out that Whitman's world may be a bold world or may be a mad world, but it is not a dislocated world because at the centre of his world dwells his own personality. This world is related to his creativity, it has its own consistency because of the 'central personal force'. It is in relation to personality that the world is a world. On the other hand the science tries to do away with personality and sets up an impersonal and unalterable standard of space and time. As a result, in science the reality of this world vanishes in an abstraction. The world of science is a world of reason but, according to Tagore, 'the reality of the world belongs to the personality of man and not to reasoning, which, useful and great though it be, is not the man himself' (Tagore 1917: 70). Illustrating his thesis with Beethoven's music, Tagore points out that if we do not understand the mystery of his music, we will then suspect the element of his personality. In a particular sonata we can make all kinds of observations, we can count the black and white keys of the keyboard, study the movement of fingers and then announce that this is Beethoven's sonata. But in the process we may forget that the origin and object of this music is grounded in the personality of the composer and that is the ultimate reality of the music. In other words for Tagore a creation takes shape through personality, personality is the reality of creation.

Tagore takes up the example of games in this regard. A game is a game when there is a player to play it. The game has its rules and regulations, but that is not the reality of the game: the game is what it is to players. The game changes its aspects according to the personality of its players: some play for gain, some for applause, others for sociality, and there are still others who approach it for curiosity; but the rules of the game remain the same. Tagore, believed that the world is like this game to us—it is the same, and yet not the same to us all. Science deals with the elements of sameness, whereas personality produces variations. Personality attains fullness in multiple relationships, in its attempt to unite with the life-world. Consciousness of personality begins with separation from the life-world and ends with the feeling of unity with all. Personality is at the root of all relations and reality is the expression of personality. For Tagore personality is the pivot of the world and if this pivot is removed, the world crumbles into abstractions. In other words personality connotes the relational being, the being-in-the-world, whose relations are nurtured, nourished and expanded in various forms. For Tagore the essential elements for the development of personality are movement and change that helps personality attain fulfilment.

Mukerji, influenced by Tagore, considered personality to be the fundamental reality of all social sciences, and maintained that every individual should be 'charged' with this reality. He thought the individual of social science is a static entity, and that the discipline is incapable of dealing with the progressive or dynamic being. For a proper conception of personality, he argued that three concepts have to be considered: 'subject', 'object' and 'reality'. He claimed the continuum between subject and object is personality. In common understanding the term 'subject' connotes the individual and his thought world and the object as the 'world of action', and there is a disjunction between the two. Mukerji on the other hand argued that the subject should always be understood in relation to the object. In other words Mukerji is arguing against the epistemological division between the mind as subject and the world as object. Against this position he argues that the fundamental reality is rather the being-in-the-world: not a subject starting from its entirely subjective consciousness and having somehow to connect with an entirely objective world, but, from the beginning a being seamlessly integrated into a world that can no more exist apart from the being than the being can exist apart from the world. That is why he says there is a unity of subject and object and this unity is represented in the *self*, so the self is more than the subject. And the self thus is also the realm of social and ethical values in existence. He writes: 'So, the dynamic element of relation and values which is not present in the common meaning of the terms subject and object, is better recognised in the concept of self' (Mukerji 2004a [1924]: 35). He believed the ethical values are transmitted through groups or society and that it is through ethics that personality can be developed. Personality, in other words, embraces multiple relationships and ethical orientations. That is why Mukerji wrote: 'If personality is developed through the establishment of relations it flourishes best in groups of men' (*ibid.*: 41). For Mukerji the core of personality is spontaneity and freedom in the sense that it is self-impelled, self-determined and self-limited. 'The "person" is a law into himself ... Personality with its activities individual and collective, with its initiatives, rights and responsibility is the be-all and end-all of all ethics' (Mukerji 2004a [1924]: 48).

For Mukerji personality is ethical because it must always mean relations. He considers the individual or citizen as theoretical abstractions and in Hegelian fashion argues that if the particular is seen in abstraction from the realm of common interests, then it cannot be ethical even if such an abstraction claims to promote the freedom of the individual. In *Philosophy of Right* Hegel has argued against desert island morality, because unless morality is mediated by society it is not aware of itself (Hegel 2010: 101–123). In other words ethics requires the co-operation of others and it is only through ethics that freedom can be realised in a plurality—in associations, and in groups. Ethnics achieved through personality as elaborated by Mukerji is truly so because here particular interests are served through social connections. It is in this sense that Mukerji calls personality moral. In his first book *Personality and the Social Sciences* (2004a [1924]) Mukerji offers a detailed and extensive critique of the concept of the individual in economic thought, political philosophy and educational theories. His basic contention was that in economics, both theoretically and practically, 'great mischief' was done by not recognising the fact that the development of personality is the central problem. The discipline valued only the individual; in their logic the economic being was an unrelated concept. Whereas for Mukerji, the relation between the individual, the economic being as he or she is called, and the personality did not strike the attention of classical economists. He considers personality as the principle of unity in diversity and takes account of the entire process, 'whereas individuality is concerned mainly with the process of competition, struggle for existence and survival of the fittest' (Mukerji 2004a [1924]: 58).

Mukerji argued that in political philosophy the same mistakes were committed as in economics. Hobbes, Locke, Hume, all of them believed that the individual was the oldest institution standing behind other institutions. Individuals had natural rights and the institutions were created to protect them. The best way to protect them was to exchange natural rights for civil rights on the condition that civil rights should retain the good points of natural rights. It seemed there was a consensus that the aim of the state was to aid the development of personality. However, according to Mukerji, theories of state were either based on gross individualism or they justified extreme individualism. This, he thought, interfered with the development of the individual and he claimed this was nothing but a dehumanised process (Mukerji 2004a [1924]: 84). In political philosophy the state is often understood as a unity, like an organism or an individual, but this unity is theorised as a mechanical unity—the state—as only a sum of individuals. Personality is either ignored here or allowed to drift along the current of self-interest and competition. Mukerji asserts that the essential postulate of individualism is that self-interest is a universal principle of human nature. In the absence of arbitrary restrictions each individual is able to do that for which s/he is best fitted. Absence of restrictions promotes free competition and such competition develops the highest human possibilities. Here Mukerji is drawing our attention to the relation between individuals and the political order from the perspective of different processes whereby the former are objectified as certain kinds of subject through the ways they are targeted by political power. Mukerji's critique here pertains more to the modern liberal and neo-liberal political thought. Mukerji argues that individuals can develop through the experience of mutual dependence and this is a part of the process of interacting with society. He describes this being as a person.

The standard description of personality in sociology refers to a set of more or less stable characteristics that distinguish one individual from another. These characteristics are assumed to hold across time and place and to underlie behaviour. The term personality therefore refers the individual as object whereas the concept of self refers to the individual as subject. Mukerji employs the idea of personality to claim that it is an enriched concept of the individual as it is developed through interaction with the collectivity or society. Following Hegel, Mukerji believes ethics requires the cooperation of others. It is only through ethics that freedom can be realised in a plurality—in associations, and in corporations. The individual is a person so long as s/he is able to work out of associations. In fact the individual derives his/her moral worth from a participation in the life of other members of society. The rights of the individual are recognised by society just as the rights and duties of the community are ensured by those of the individual. Mukerji writes: 'So, the inter-relation between the life of the individual and that of other members of the society is the condition of morality' (2004a [1924]: 211).

But he discarded the idea of 'group-mind' as a super-individual, superior, mystical entity, though he accepted the 'legal personality' of groups. He therefore argues that the relationship between an individual and a group or collectivity is not one of interaction between the individual and traditions, 'but simply one of development of personality resident in an individual who creates and recreates the traditional values. But the individual dies sooner than traditions, though personality persists' (Mukerji 2004a [1924]: 234). Personality provides uniqueness and concreteness to the individual and because of its capacity for inter-penetration, the individual acquires the capability to develop. So, according to Mukerji, the test of ideal group-life is whether personality is developing through it or not, because group-life very often obstructs such development. He writes: 'The development of Personality includes both [static and dynamic] points of view; thus, it starts from the individual, acts through the group and yet transcends it. Personality is not exhausted by creating groups, it harmonises them through the individuals realising themselves through the groups' (*ibid.*: 241–242).

Mukerji believed that social science remained tied to the concept of the truncated, static individual, forgetting that the individual was the potential personality. He considered personality as a dynamic principle developing through knowledge and action. The individual can at best be the starting point of social science. In ethics as well the individual can only be the starting point; the group is the means through which the individual will create the end when s/he will emphasise the development of the individual's own personality more than his or her selfish impulses. Mukerji concludes his essay with the following words:

> Now, a science of society is concerned with the individual and the group, though it is said to be more concerned with the group than with the individual. But a group consists of individuals who are dependent upon one another. There are two orders of facts here—an individual's own world, either his own inheritance, his own acquirements, and the fact of interdependence. Sociology as yet is concerned with the facts of interdependence. So, it is now only a science of a group; its exclusiveness will have to be cured by coordinating it with the "science" of Personality. Individualisation is interwoven with socialisation inevitably and synthesis is Personality. This is how we understand sociology. (Mukerji 2004a [1924]: 303)

In *Basic Concepts in Sociology* (2004b [1932]) Mukerji again comes back to the theme of personality which he now describes as the synthesis of 'sociality and individuality' (*ibid.*: 85). Discussing the question of equality and social justice Mukerji points out that the individual as s/he lives today in society is 'full of mental knots, thorns and gnarls', whereas equality is only possible among *persons*, that is, when the individuals rise to their full nature. In other words the ideal of equality is a symbol of personality, a test of social justice. He claims that

Indian society had its own ways of developing into 'persons'. In fact it was essentially not much different from Western ideas: it meant achievement of harmony by making a *persona*, that is development of a being in conformity with external reality. But Mukerji adds: 'The difference has been in the culture rather than in the content of the idea. The Hindu sages laid stress on self-culture and intuition, chiefly, by association with gurus in preference to control or ratiocination' (2004b [1932]: 185). Mukerji believed that the Indian mind has an irresistible appeal for the principles of *shantam, shivam, advaitam* (harmony, welfare, unity) and only when 'the individual begins consciously to realise the threefold principle that life becomes fully charged with meaning. In and through such realisation the life of the individual attains its personality' (*ibid.*: 46). He thinks of personality as the subjective organisation of a person's consciousness recreated through introspection along with other forms of knowledges and social practices.

Purusha and Personhood

In his first book *Personality and the Social Sciences* (2004a [1924]), Mukerji's mode of argument against the individual is technical and academic. In his Bengali writings he is much more forthright and straightforward in his critique. He adopts this style mainly because in Bengali he is writing for non-technical, general readers and makes his point directly. Actually it is in these writings that he gradually introduces the concept of *purusha*. In his early writings *Amra o Tahara* ('Us and Them', 1931), he wrote that everyone understands the individual as an inner object and society as an outer object, but in this so called inner and outer objects there is a continuum. Since this continuum is related with the individual it is concrete and its character is universal. This continuum is known as personality. In his collection of Bengali essays (written between 1947 and 1949) entitled *Byaktabya* ('Utterance', 1957) he discusses in greater detail his reservations about the concept of the individual.

He believed the individual was born in the West as a product of Renaissance humanism. As a part of the expansion of trade and commerce, the individual was entrusted with qualities such as enterprise, adventure, drive. He thought the result of the birth of the individual was disastrous for the West. According to Mukerji what we understand by European culture began to decline from the time of the Renaissance itself. He wrote:

> The basis of culture is not the individual but the community or *samaj* (society) as Hindus call it. When the sense of community is lost, the need of nationalism arises to fill up the empty space. Just as an individual is one, so too a nation is one; just as an individual is adventurous for the sake of gain, so too is a nation desirous of extending its power. Nation gives rise to the national state, and even as this is in the making, the individual is sought to be restrained—for such is the nature of the collective. The individual protests in the name of freedom by seeking to obtain control of the state. (Mukerji 1957: 9; Munshi 2009: 37–38)

It was during this time he began to think of an alternative to the concept of the individual, which he thought was the bane of Western society. He proposed the idea of the 'person' or '*purusha*' who develops through interaction and praxis. The individual is alienated, estranged from society, whereas *purusha* has multiple relations with society. He wrote: 'Man will have to be *purusha*. He cannot be an individual or single entity. He has to be a person' (Mukerji 1957: 17; Munshi 2009: 43).

Mukerji believed individualism could only produce nihilism and blatant greed for power and this was his critique of the West. His perception for man in the new society was his faith in *purusha,* and evolving and unfettered human subjectivity related to and developing out of the social matrix. This was his prescription for the new society of independent India where faith in man can only mean faith in the *purusha*. Mukerji specifically points out that the term *purusha* he advocates is not the same as the *purusha* of the *Sankhya* or that of the *Gita*. However there is a similarity as well between it and the *purushakara,* in the sense that one relies on one's own powers in order to liberate oneself voluntarily from the domination of the cycle of nature and the cycle of *karma*. He points out that there is significant difference between individualism and personalism (*purushavad*): 'The first difference is that the individual is estranged from society and hence he becomes an enemy of society or socially frustrated, alienated being' (Mukerji 1957: 18; Munshi 2009: 44). This sense of estrangement manifests itself in loneliness, anti-social activities and meaningless criticism and opposition. 'The obscurity in poetry, the self-conceit of scientists and artists, the egoism of specialists and the self-satisfaction of social reformers are all manifestations of the contradiction that is inherent in individualism' (Mukerji 1957: 19; Munshi 2009: 44–45). What is this contradiction or opposition? Mukerji locates it in the logic of 'either/or', which according to him originates from the principle of individualism. On the other hand *purushavad* does not have this 'versus-sense'; it is integrative and assimilative in principle. That is why he wrote: '*cooperative, affiliative purusha is real, the individual is unreal*' (Mukerji 1957: 20, italics mine). For him the essence of man's social being lies in this reality. That is why *purusha* wants to create extended relation, association, alliance, companionship, cooperation, cohabitation, where its humanity can be tested. The *purusha* is autonomous and different from the asocial personality of the West. And this is the reason why *purusha* is eager to earn his rights and discharge his responsibilities. In *purusha* both rights and duties combine.

Purushavad reconciles another contradiction, which is the opposition between tradition and experimentation. It is generally believed that those who follow tradition are conservative and those who experiment are progressive. But Mukerji asserts: 'A person is born in the womb of tradition and on the strength of his works he comes out into life's testing grounds. The same human being bears the burden of tradition and moves forward, sometimes lessening the burden and sometimes taking up new burdens without any qualms' (Mukerji 1957: 25; Munshi 2009: 49). He believed that however disintegrated Indian society might have become it has not turned into a garbage heap of 'discrete individual atoms'. In its mode of behaviour, attitudes and practices we find a concept of man that is more conducive to *purushavad* than individualism. Pointing out the difference between the Western and Indian images of man, Mukerji writes: 'if we have to choose between the deductive, fragmented, floating, rootless and in that sense independent individualism of European societies, and the integrated, concrete, and in that sense norm regulated, human beings of Indian civilisation then we can assuredly go for the traditional way' (Mukerji 1957: 25; Munshi 2009: 49). He wrote that the way he understood Marxism, it had something similar to this kind of *purushavad*. He believed the 'individual' is a huge abstraction originating in the age of capitalism in England. The basis of individualism is economic progress. *Purushavad* encourages the development of man within social habitat.

Alternative Concept of Man

In his reflections written in the form of a diary entitled *Jhilimili* ('Twinkling' 1965 [1961]), Mukerji wrote in 1958 that the main theme of his writings had always been what is called personality (dated 22.5.1958). However, as we have seen, his idea of personality changed over time and it is possible to see its final culmination in his Presidential Address to the Indian Sociological Conference in 1955. In this lecture he points out that the unit of the Indian social system is not the 'individual as actor' and action for the Indian is not individualistic or voluntaristic. Instead it is structured on a normative system of coordinates. Since the social system is normative in orientation there is no escape from tradition for an Indian. Here the group is still the unit of action and normative orientation, but Mukerji points out that this system is not devoid of freedom. 'Our conception of freedom is different, because our conception of man is *purusha* and *not* the individual, or *vyakti*' (Mukerji 2002 [1958]: 269). He perceptively observes that the paraphernalia of the modern state coerces us to 'belong to a "free" society of individuals, each exercising his right of choice despite advertisements, press-chains, chain-stores, and empty purse too, which, you must admit, does not leave much scope for "consumer's sovereignty"' (*ibid.*).

It is clear that Mukerji's search for a sociology of personality was in a sense a search for an alternative concept of man which was not based on individualism. Reading Western modernity on the logic of individualism, Mukerji thought it had bleak prospects for the future of man. His idea of *purusha* was, in fact, a search for an advanced, enriched, enhanced and developed concept of man who has ethical orientation and who enjoys freedom. It was a search for a new image of man. Mukerji was critical of Western humanism as he believed that the concept of the individual was born as a consequence of Renaissance humanism. Mukerji was an anti-humanist so far as Western humanism was concerned; even so he believed that his idea of *purushavad* could provide a firm foundation for a different kind of humanism. He called this neo-humanism (Mukerji 1957). However, I think he was mistaken in his attempt to rescue humanism in some form, and that instead he should have discarded this project altogether. His anti-humanist theory of personality would have been more radical and contemporary.

Mukerji also produced an early critique of what Foucault called the 'society of normalisation' in his Bengali book *Chintayasi* ('Reflect'! 1933). Mukerji believed that the view of man as a dissocialised being follows from the individualistic conception of man who is capable of constituting himself independently of any relation to society, as a subject without intersubjectivity. On the other hand, in Mukerji's idea of *purusha*, society and intersubjectivity are two crucial elements.

The epistemic structure of early Indian sociology represented by Mukerji and others was not simply constructed in opposition to the abstract typologies of social structure and ahistoricity of Western sociology. Positively, it argued for an alternate image of man, a conception of man different from the idea of the individual where man becomes man only among men. This man is not an abstract, isolated, 'dehumanised' individual, but acquires personality in the society of other men.

Personality in this scheme endorses an idea of a subjectivity appearing as such only in response to the other. In his novels like *Antashila* ('Subterranean', 1935), *Abarta* ('Eddy', 1937) and *Mohana* ('Estuary', 1943), Mukerji tried to show how personality evolves through engagement with the surrounding community and through commitment to action. In his theory of personality, man's agency thus acquires significance. In constituting himself or herself as the person, the individual relies on interaction with other people, history and culture. In short Mukerji argues for efforts towards self-transformation to escape the hazards of a society of dehumanised, desocialised individuals.

Louis Dumont also subscribes to the anti-modernist view and critiques the hyper-individualistic consummation of modernity in the West (Dumont 1986). He, like Mukerji, is critical of the obliteration of man-to-man relation by modernity in favour of a mere man-to-things relation. For Dumont this relationship encourages the isolationist view of man as an individual without considering his relation to others in a community. He views modern society as atomised where man's regard for others is eclipsed by regard for his relations to things. On this account Dumont declares his preference for hierarchy, expressing a certain repugnance towards individualistic/modern desocialisation (*ibid.*: 60, 267). He assumes that the only way of conceiving the man-to-man relation is from the hierarchical perspective of holism. Dumont thus manifestly confuses *intersubjectivity* with *interdependence* and can conceive of the former only on the model of the latter. But must we accept his certainty that the only form of subjectivity, the only imaginable modality for recognising the other, is hierarchical interdependence?

Mukerji escapes Dumont's predicament and in fact, provides a better alternative by focusing on *purusha* or 'person' who is interactive, integrative with collectivity and self-transformative. In this integrative mode *purusha* negotiates between rights and responsibilities, between tradition and experiment, attempts to achieve a set of collective goals and charts out a route for self-transition. What is important in this exercise is Mukerji's refusal to accept the ideology of individualism as something beneficial to society and man. It is possible to locate inconsistencies and gaps in Mukerji's theoretical structure, but what is not possible to deny is his refusal to accept the individual and the reduction of the destiny of modern societies to the playing out of individualism. When Mukerji characterised Western societies as a 'garbage-heap of individual atoms' he thereby refused to accept the idea of *progress* inherent in the transition from a holistic to an individualistic culture. He was perceptive enough to recognise that the emergence of individualism was liable to be accompanied by certain negativities like the atomisation of society, an indifference to politics, obsession with consumption and the like. Mukerji notes with concern the formidable thrust of individualistic existences and aspirations in the West resulting in a relational impasse, a crisis in communication breakdown of the community, deficit in intersubjective communication and anaemic social relations. By positing person/*purusha* Mukerji provides an alternative sociology of man who is relational, integrative, linked to tradition and because of such multiple connections he is ethical. Mukerji even attributes freedom in the manner a person emerges, in his metaphor, like a silkworm cutting through its own cocoon. Mukerji accepts that in his scheme of things collectivity is considered as a unit of action; therefore, aspiration, normative orientation and the possibility of Indian social life being regimented and regulated cannot be denied. He writes:

> I almost accept that argument ... but ... the majority of us do *not* feel regimented. In fact, quite a number of honest and true men have felt free ... our conception of freedom is different, because our conception man is *purusha* and not the individual, or *vyakti*. I wonder how many times the word *vyakti* occurs in our religious texts. (Mukerji 2002 [1958]: 269)

It is possible to discern an intuitive conception of freedom in Mukerji's argument, but what is important to note that Mukerji intended to locate the realm of freedom not in the individual but in the *purusha*.

Overcoming Individualism

Max Weber's complaint was that the term 'individualism' was imprecise. He said that 'it includes the most heterogeneous things imaginable'. We can agree with Weber that in view of the term's vast conceptual range, 'a thorough analysis of these concepts in historical terms would at the present time be highly valuable to science' (Weber 1958: 222). Dumont points out that much imprecision and difficulty arises from failing to distinguish in the 'individual' the empirical agent and the rational being and normative subject of institutions (Dumont 1970 [1966]: 8–9). A proper understanding of individualism is necessary for the knowledge of contemporary modernity. Mukerji also brings out various imprecisions in the idea of the individual in his writings as we have seen. He ultimately rejects the individual and thereby rejects the trajectory of Western modernity; he also rejects Western humanism. He believes that instead of the rootless, fragmented, floating and, in some sense, independent individuals of the West, the norm-regulated, integrated, rooted, concrete human beings of India are a better option.

For Mukerji the individual is the fictitious atom of an 'ideological' representation of society. As contemporary thinkers like Foucault point out, the individual is also fabricated by a technology of power called 'discipline'. In the contemporary expanding arena of the modern Western state and its administrative apparatus, human beings within a given domain were considered a resource. The individual was of interest exactly insofar as s/he could contribute to the strength of the state. Modern thought views humans as individual subjects. This aspect of the emergence of the modern individual as an object of political and scientific concern was unacceptable to Mukerji. The modern individual, as Foucault would say, is the effect and object of a certain crossing of power and knowledge. Power techniques are oriented towards individuals and intended to rule them in a continuous and permanent way. Mukerji and his contemporary sociologists' early critiques attack the idea of the individual, which is for them isolationist, breaks links with others, splits up community life, forces the individual back on himself and ties him down to his own identity. These are, in many ways, contemporary concerns, and anticipate the current struggle against the 'government of individualisation'. The important problem of our times then is not to try to liberate the individual from the state and its institutions, but as Mukerji's search for an alternative to the individual and individuation shows, the social and philosophical compulsion is to find ways to liberate humans both from the state and from the kind of individualisation which is linked to the state. What is needed is a process of 'de-individualisation' through collectivities and diverse combinations. There is a need to promote new forms of subjectivity through the refusal of this kind of individuality, and this Mukerji attempts to do with his theory of personhood.

Persons are products of socio-cultural conditions; individuals exist in spite of them. Persons may be understood as those who realise the given and embody the categories which are prescribed by tradition and the social order. The person is continuously in process of elaboration and producing himself or herself through social action and interaction. Most importantly the person's freedom includes reasoned agreement to the norms of common life; personal identity is formed and maintained in reciprocal relations with others and group memberships contribute to self-fulfilment. Thus Mukerji stresses the social dimension of autonomy and practices of freedom in contrast to dissocialised individuals. The person is aware of himself or herself as a social being; s/he perceives her personality as tied to the knowledges, language, tradition, attitude and gestures whose images are reflected by the collectivity. Since Mukerji considered personality as a dynamic principle developing through knowledge and action, in a reflexive gesture he links his theoretical insight to the development of his *own* personality and writes:

> I had come to [sociology] because, being interested in developing my personality through knowledge, I realised that none of the social or the natural sciences I had to study in my earlier days could give me, at one and the

> same time, the synoptic view, the large vision and the understanding of the milieu of knowledge which were necessary for the fulfilment of my being. It has all been a personal affair, not a matter of sociology for the sake of sociology. (Mukerji 2002 [1958]: 261)

In reaction against the individualistic drift of humanism, Mukerji thus attempts at a re-composition of the subject and re-inventing man. His overcoming of individualism is thus to be understood as an attempt to overthrow the monadologial perspective of modern Western sociology.

FOUR

NIRMAL KUMAR BOSE (1901–1972)

Interpreting Man and Society: A Cultural-Historical Perspective

Anthropology and the Paradigm of Science

In 1946 when Nirmal Kumar Bose was accompanying Gandhi on his tour of riot-torn Noakhali, 'an interesting conversation' took place between the two:

> He [Gandhi] called me .... and asked me if I did not at all believe in God. I confessed that the problem whether God existed or not, or what was the primal cause of the universe, had never seriously come into my life. I did not concern myself with the question of such ultimates.
>
> "Don't you believe in anything?" he asked.
>
> I said, "Yes, as a scientist, I do believe in truth. For, in the laboratory or in our scientific investigations, we undoubtedly try to discover the truth by observation and experiment. Unless we believe that there's something worth striving for, why should we engage in the chase at all? Truth may be like a carrot dangling before a donkey's nose, but it is there all the same."
>
> Gandhiji said, "that will do". (Bose 1974: 49–50)

A few days later, when similar questions cropped up, Bose says: 'I told him how scientific research was my true vocation (*swadharma*) while serving in the political campaign, even when it was by intellect was no more than an emergency duty (*apadharma*)' (Bose 1974: 67). Bose's conviction that he was engaged as a scientist in scientific pursuit also reflects his understanding of anthropology, which he always considered a branch of science.

Surajit Sinha, one of Bose's former students and a close acquaintance, writes: 'As a younger anthropologist who had been in touch with Professor Bose for over twenty years I have often felt that he was a little too obsessed with presenting himself as a "scientist"' (Sinha 1986: 45). It is no surprise that Bose shared in the twentieth-century discourse of anthropology as a science, emphasising a limited subject focus, in-depth fieldwork, codified data accumulation, and cautiously restricted inferences. He was deeply influenced by Franz Boas and considered him one of his gurus in anthropology (Sinha 1973: 1). Unlike earlier evolutionary theorists, who had emphasised overall cultural similarities, Boas stressed the differences and particularity of each culture as a result of its specific and divergent historical development. It is well known that Boas was critical of the tendency in anthropology towards premature generalisation and speculative history, arguing in favour of the meticulous collection ('total recovery') of ethnographic data before generalisation could be attempted. Anthropology, Boas believed, must ultimately discover some laws, just as any proper science must, but such laws could not be discovered until all the evidence was in. Since all the evidence would never be in, the anthropologist, now a kind of 'connoisseur of chaos', had best stick to particularities and defer concern for pattern or general lawfulness. What impressed Bose most about Boas, he told Sinha, was his inductive natural history approach which kept the mind open to unexpected discovery: 'Boas started with observations and then moved towards classification and generalisation rather than starting with a deductive hypothetical model' (Sinha 1973: 1). This is the characteristic claim of the science of empiricism in which induction is considered the indispensable foundation of all factual knowledge.

By implication here, ethnography is a neutral, tropeless discourse that renders and recovers in a 'scientific' language other realities 'exactly as they are'. This language somehow bypasses values and interpretive schema. The language of science has traditionally excluded certain expressive modes from its repertoire such as subjectivity (in the name of objectivity), rhetoric (in the name of 'plain', transparent signification), and fiction (in the name of fact) (Clifford 1986a: 5). The qualities eliminated from science were localised in the category of 'literature'. Whatever may have been the case in other sciences, in ethnography the crucial problem was to reconcile the 'contradiction ... between personal and scientific authority', a contradiction that had taken an acute turn 'since the advent of fieldwork as methodological norm' (Pratt 1986: 32). James Clifford says: 'Anthropological field work has been represented as both a scientific "laboratory" and a personal "rite of passage". The two metaphors capture nicely the discipline's impossible attempt to fuse objective and subjective practices' (Clifford 1986b: 109). It has been argued that ethnographic texts are not simply objective descriptions of reality but are constituted in terms of a set of problematic links between ethnographic authority, personal experience, scientism, and literary style. Personal experiences of fieldwork, often narrated at the beginning of the text, produce a kind of authority that is located in the subjective experience of the ethnographer (Pratt 1986: 27–50). However, a formal text has to conform to the rules of a scientific discourse whose authority demands that the speaking and the experiencing subject be effaced. Tensions between these competing authorities are inscribed in all ethnographic texts. As Pratt points out, 'There are strong reasons why field ethnographers so often lament that their ethnographic writings leave out or hopelessly impoverish some of the most important knowledge they have achieved, including the self-knowledge' (*ibid.*: 33).

We witness a similar tension in Bose's writings, exacerbated by his claims to being a scientist, even as he was aware of the sensuous and experiential side of his fieldwork. Bose was never only an anthropologist; he wrote on social history, art, politics, temple architecture, archaeology, geology, human geography, education, social work, nationalism, and Gandhism. He also wrote prolifically in Bengali—many of his Bengali essays are in the form of travelogues, autobiographical sketches, personal narratives, and social portraitures anchored in personal experience. These were published in journals like *Prabasi, Desh, Sanibarer Chithi,* and *Sahitya Parisad Patrika,* and later included in two remarkable collections, *Paribrajaker Diary* ('A Wanderer's Diary', Bose 1982 [1940]) and *Nabin o Prachin* ('The New and the Old', Bose 1949 [1930]). In these writings we find personal accounts, at the time considered inconsequential and trivial, occupying a privileged place. In these accounts Bose sets himself free, as it were, from the objectifying demands of scientific discourse and establishes his personal authority on the texts. Here the narrator is not self-effacing, nor simply a hand that writes—as is expected in formal-scientific description. We witness in these expressive and literary writings an anthropologist who is subverting his own 'science'. I argue later that this is particularly related to the vernacularisation of ethnography, in which Bose played a pioneering role. Before that, however, it is essential to present a general outline of Bose's life and anthropology.

Culture and Cultural Traits

Nirmal Kumar Bose (1901–1971) was a scholar of wide-ranging interests, an indefatigable fieldworker, a person deeply committed to Gandhian ideals and a great nationalist. He studied geology at Presidency College, Calcutta, and in 1921 joined the same college for a M.Sc. degree in geology. His studies were interrupted during the Non-cooperation Movement when Bose decided to abandon his studies to join the movement. Moving to Puri with his mother around this time, he also developed an interest in the architecture and sculptures of the temples of Orissa. Soon he started giving lectures on the temples and their architecture to visitors. Asutosh Mukherjee, then vice-chancellor of Calcutta University, was present at one of these lectures and was very impressed with the clarity of Bose's exposition. He persuaded Bose to come to the university, suggesting that he begin with courses at the new department of anthropology then being built up. He pointed out to Bose that, with his training in geology and knowledge of temple architecture, he would find the course challenging. Mukherjee emphasised that Bose should not equate Calcutta University with a government department. Bose joined the Department of Anthropology in 1923 for a postgraduate degree, graduating in 1925. This was followed by a research fellowship to study the Juangs of Pal Lahara. In the field Bose found himself distressed by dilemmas when he witnessed that all Juangs were undernourished and suffering from malaria (Bose 1949 [1930]: 18–19; Sinha 1986: 13). Bose's experience with the Juangs convinced him that academic research alone was not enough, and that knowledge must also be used for social welfare. In 1930 he left the university to join Gandhi's salt *satyagraha* movement and was arrested in 1931. During this time, Bose began a serious study of Gandhian literature, spending part of his time in jail thinking and writing about Gandhi, an experience which later culminated in *Selections from Gandhi* (Bose 1934).

In 1937 Syamaprasad Mukherjee, then vice-chancellor of Calcutta University, persuaded Bose to join the Department of Anthropology as assistant lecturer. Bose taught prehistoric archaeology to undergraduate and postgraduate classes. A great believer in fieldwork, in 1939 he arranged for his students to be involved in archaeological excavations at Kuliana in Mayurbhanj. He was soon able to build up a large collection of Palaeolithic tools for the prehistory unit of the department. During this period he wrote about prehistoric research in Mayurbhanj (Bose 1940a), as well as on Gandhi (Bose 1940b). In August 1942 when the Quit India movement was launched, Bose was arrested again. He was released only in 1945, after three and a half years. Upon his release he regained his old job as assistant lecturer in the Anthropology Department. In 1946 he was offered a position of lecturer in human geography at the Department of Geography. In 1967 he became the Commissioner for the Scheduled Castes and Scheduled Tribes and prepared several reports which bear his distinction. However, from 1971 Bose began showing signs of illness and was found to be suffering from cancer. Even during his illness, when he was virtually confined to bed, he continued his writing and participated in a number of important meetings and discussions. He died in October 1972.

Bose's early anthropology, including *Cultural Anthropology* (1929), was influenced by Boas and Kroeber's cross-cultural analysis. The method of Boas was known as continuous area cross-cultural analysis. This type of analysis samples the available data within a specified region, enabling controls to be exercised for geographical, linguistic, and environmental relations. Early studies of this kind by Kroeber and his students took societies as the units of analysis, and compared inventories of traits in order to elaborate 'cultural similarity matrices'. Bose was particularly attracted to this approach because he believed that a proper understanding of Indian civilisation would require anthropologists to go beyond the study of tribal communities. In the culture-area approach, and in theories of diffusion and cross-cultural comparison, the concept of the 'cultural trait', which Bose discusses in great detail with numerous Indian examples in *Cultural Anthropology*, is of central importance. His early work on the spring festival of India, an important study of the diffusion of cultural traits, defines the geographical area covered by this cultural trait at any period in its history as extending from the eastern provinces of India to Europe (Bose 1927: 112–155). In this richly illustrated essay, Bose argues that one of the festival's chief centres of dispersal lay in eastern India, where the original form of the festival was perpetuated by the Nagas, Kandhs, and Oraons, and is observed in its purest form in Bengal, Bihar, Orissa and among the Gonds of the Central Provinces. Bose later applied the theory of the diffusion of cultural traits to his work on temple architecture and material culture in rural India.

André Béteille points out that, much before Dumont and Pocock, Bose realised the importance of combining ethnology and Indology in the study of Indian society (Béteille 1975). But for him an anthropology of tribes that merely confirmed the Indological perspective was not sufficient since tribal society had changed following the advent of colonialism. Thus, Bose attempted to integrate history into his scheme, not only to enhance the analysis of social change but also for social reconstruction. His book on cultural anthropology begins:

> The social structure which we have inherited from the past was built in answer to the challenge of certain problems of life, many of which are now out of action. A new set of problems has arisen in the course of the last twenty years, and it is no longer possible to live according to the old ways under modern conditions. A determined effort should therefore be made to adapt our cultural heritage to present day needs and requirements. In this work of reconstruction, many thinkers believe the social sciences will be of great service to humanity. (Bose 1953 [1929]: 1)

This particular idea of social science resembled in many ways the practices of applied science. Bose believed that this science could help in understanding the 'mechanics of the working of human history' in the same way as diagrams and charts help an engineer understand the structure and operations of an engine. As a science, anthropology is not capable of building up hope in man or regenerating faith where none exists; but, in a limited fashion, anthropology can always analyse a society's present in terms of its past, draw out the factors responsible for change, and enable both scientific development and social reconstruction. This view of anthropology developed later in the post-War years as applied or development anthropology, whose practitioners accepted the need and desire for change in the developing world. In this apolitical view, focused on cultural differences, the national political structure is basically benevolent. Such a view obscures the fact that it is often structures of social and politico-economic dominance which create developmental problems. Bose's view of the role of anthropology in moulding reconstruction and development is similarly problematic, as we shall see.

In *Cultural Anthropology* Bose defines the central problem of anthropology in terms of evolution of culture and its relation with man's physical evolution. He illustrates his idea of culture by taking Vaishnavism in Bengal as a concrete example. He points out that the Vaishnav religion consists of habitual actions, attitudes and sentiments centred on the idea of a particular god, a specific organisation of sect marked by food, dress and ceremonies. While defining what he means by a cultural trait, Bose first points out the differences in dress, food habits and religion in various provinces of India, and explains that the units of culture in each province are different; each of these distinguishing units he calls a trait. He believes that the study of cultural traits gives a convenient means of judging the influence of one culture over another, and of finding the path of diffusion of a particular trait. The continuity of a specific culture depends upon the transmission of such traits. The task of an anthropologist is to map the distribution of cultural traits, locate the 'cultural province' of a trait, study the modification of a trait and to determine the overall course of historical change. This type of analysis, however, suffers from limitations determined by the assumption which the investigator builds into his model, and from the problems involved in making historical inferences from synchronic data.

A deeper problem relates to the cultural relativist position that was associated with Boas and his followers. It implies that the concept of culture is invoked by anthropologists as an explanatory principle which can account for all differences and forms of behaviour in human groups. The dominance of the culture concept can often lead to the neglect of the analysis of social, political and economic structures and processes. For example, studies of cultural contact and change attributed to cultural differences can often be the result of conflicting political and economic interests or contradictions between different classes or groups. But Bose in his anthropology was not oblivious to such factors. Theories of cultural contacts through diffusion view cultures as patchwork of borrowed traits, the superior traits moving out from the centre, like the ripples from a stone thrown into a pond. The movement of these cultural traits could be reconstructed by assuming that the traits most widely distributed are the oldest. Anthropology has largely moved away from this orientation, seeing most cultural traits in disparate areas as having developed independently and criticising the diffusionists for extracting cultural artefacts from their context. Though acculturation studies maintain an interest in the process whereby cultural elements may be transferred from one group to another and the manner in which such elements are transformed and adopted to their new context. Bose, in fact, analysed the process of absorption of tribes into Hindu society in terms of acculturation, as we shall see. While commenting on the Hindu mode of acculturation Bose observed that economic relations played a crucial role in the sphere of social and cultural relations, as culture flowed from a politically and economically dominant group to a subservient one.

Bose's central emphasis was on culture, which he understood in terms of cultural traits. Though cultural traits can be classified into a number of groups, they are intimately related to one another, and change in one produces change in all the other groups. For Bose, the outward form of culture was conditioned by human experience and changed with time. In his analysis of culture he attempted to classify Indian culture in terms of a three-fold *dharma*, namely *artha-dharma*, *kama-dharma*, and *moksha-dharma*. Each of these dharmas, he explained, acts in four phases, namely (i) *vastu* or material object; (ii) *kriya* or habitual action; (iii) *samhati* or social grouping; and (iv) *tattva* or knowledge. Further, *tattva* can again be sub-classified into two groups depending on whether the knowledge is *vichar-mulaka*, i.e., based on criticism, or *viswas-mulaka*, i.e., based on faith. He followed a similar course in describing the religious culture of Bengal and characterised one of the principal religious cults of Bengal, namely Vaishnavism, in terms of various *bhavas* (attitudes), such as *sakhya* (friendship), *dasya* (service), *sanskara* (convention), and various *gunas* (Bose 1953 [1929]: 13–20).

Subsequently, Bose applied his cultural analysis to demarcate the cultural zones of India, attempting to show that the regions or states of India, though separated by differences of language, share many elements of material as well as high culture. He attributed this to diffusion. From a culturalist perspective, India emerges in Bose's writings as a place where a superior order of cultural unity prevails: 'Thus, in spite of the fact that languages of India are many, and there are well marked differences between one regional culture and another, yet there is an overall unity of design which makes them all members of one family.... The details might vary from place to place ... yet the sameness of traditions on which all of them have been reared cannot be overlooked' (Bose 1967: 9).

Bose summarised his thematic approach to cultural anthropology in the following manner: first, institutions are crystallised manifestations of the behaviour of communities. Second, persons adapt themselves to their 'cultural inheritance—or social structure, as some would prefer to call it' and in the process alter that structure as well. 'And it is this interplay between life and culture which maintains culture in a state of dynamic equilibrium' (Bose 1967: v). Hence, for Bose, the human element is an important operative factor in cultural evolution. It is here that Bose differed in important ways from Kroeber's influential ideas about 'the superorganic', which involved the complete subordination of the individual to his cultural milieu (Kroeber 1971: 163–213). Bose, on the other hand, believed that at certain moments in history creative and deviant individuals may be the starting point of change (Sinha 1973: 2).

Since both history and change remained two very important constituents of Bose's thinking on anthropology, he appropriated anthropological theories only after suitable modification. Bose's *Cultural Anthropology* was published a few years after the functionalist ethnographies of Malinowski and Radcliffe-Brown, but before functionalism had emerged as a coherent body of theory. Though one also finds mention in his work of the 'adaptive function of culture', Bose's understanding of function was not ahistorical in nature (Bose 1953 [1929]: 8–12). On the contrary he focused on adaptation in the context of historical change. He believed that historical developments were associated with a number of unresolved problems. If the cultural heritage was found inadequate in serving these needs, certain modifications – characterised as 'adaptive functions' – were bound to occur. It must be remembered that, within early twentieth-century anthropology, there were two approaches: a broadly geographical approach, which was concerned with migration, cultural diffusion, and the classification of peoples and objects; and what was generally called the sociological approach, which dealt with the development of social institutions, such as caste. The former sort of anthropologists tended to be more descriptive and particularistic, while the latter were more comparative and theoretical. Bose was an exponent of both varieties of anthropology. He continued to rely on some form of diffusionism, expressed in the careful historical-geographical analysis of the relationships between cultures and culture areas. And he employed his sociological ideas productively in one particular field within which he remains a pioneer, namely, studies of architecture.

Architecture and the Representation of Cultural Categories

Even today there are relatively few explorations of the relationship between architecture and anthropology, despite the fact that this is a field of great potential interest for the anthropologist, representing as it does an interface between ideology and technology. Human dwellings and settlements reflect both the needs and constraints imposed by the environment and the mode of subsistence, and the society's concept of individual, family, and communal life. From his early days, Bose showed keen interest in the architecture of the land, especially the architectural style of tribals and peasants. Architectural design both reflects and shapes people's expectations of the environment and the use of its resources. Among people with relatively little technological development, dwellings and communities may be more impermanent than in a modern city, but they display the dynamic interplay between materials, environment, and man's ideal models of family and social life. In his early work, Bose makes this careful observation about Bengal architecture:

> West Bengal has an original style of domestic architecture. The roof of the cottage is thatched with straw and the outline of the ridge-pole and caves is convex. The shape of the thatches is also slightly spherical ... not flat and straight as in Orissa or East Bengal.... Although temples in West Bengal are not made of earth like the cottages but of bricks, yet there is a resemblance between the two ... The temples are sometimes made more elaborate by placing two roofs side by side or by putting them one over another with a short height of wall interposing between them. ... [and] when turrets are set at each corner of the roof. (Bose 1953 [1929]: 16–17)

He further goes on to observe that 'the Bengali type of hut becomes rarer' as you travel towards Chotanagpur. Near Jhalda, between the headquarters of Manbhum and Ranchi, 'the number of typical Bengali huts is evenly matched with the tiled huts of Bihar' (*ibid.*). Moving farther west, 'the curved and thatched roof disappears altogether' to give way to 'the straight and tiled' cottages (*ibid.*). And in Chotanagpur, one rarely sees temples in the Bengali style.

Though Bose's principal interest in commenting on domestic architecture was to demonstrate the distribution of cultural traits, his meticulous description also illustrates how ethno-architectural principles reflect important social and cultural categories and relationships, for example, the symbolism that identifies a house with a lineage, and so on. In an essay on the Birhors, Bose showed how the Birhors maintained a distinctive house-building style, with a circular ground plan and a conical roof. He related this pattern to the migratory lifestyle of the Birhors, who find it easier to build a conical hut with no separate walls. But he complicated the issue by pointing out that many low castes of Andhra Pradesh, near Waltair, had circular houses with conical roofs, while at least three castes of northern Gujarat, namely Rewari, Mer, and Waghri, built completely circular, mud-wall huts, surmounted by a pointed, conical thatched roof (Bose 1967: 172). Bose was continuously drawing attention to such details of domestic architecture and seeking explanations.

This interest in domestic architecture developed out of his interest in temple architecture. When Bose left Presidency College in 1921 in response to Gandhi's call, and began living in Puri, he became interested in the architecture and sculptures of the temples of Puri, Konarak, and Bhubaneswar and began enquiries about the basic architectural principles of these temples. He met a group of *silpis,* the traditional stone carvers and temple builders, and through them came across certain manuscripts which he translated with annotations in the book *Canons of Orissan Architecture* (Bose 1932). He also wrote a number of articles and a book in Bengali on this subject, *Konaraker Bibaran* ('Description of Konarak', Bose 1960a [1926]). Bose distinguished his approach from a standard architectural one by pointing out that Western scholars and their Indian disciples were trained in European schools of architecture and never looked at Indian buildings from the Indian craftsman's perspective. 'They did not know how buildings and temples were classified by the builders themselves, what distinctions were drawn between different varieties of temples, which were considered the finer points in building-technique and so forth' (Bose 1932: 1). This also shows Bose's unwavering interest in constructing a form of knowledge in terms of indigenous categories. He studied categories of Oriya architecture with the help of local craftsmen and supplemented this by fieldwork in different parts of Orissa. Thus, Bose writes: 'A workable restoration of the science of architecture in Orissa has been secured. When similar restorations are available for other provinces in India and the existing examples of architecture studied in their light, it will be possible to reconstruct the history of Indian architecture with some degree of certainty' (Bose 1932: 4).

What must have interested Bose in these canons is not simply that these texts presented the craftsmen's perspective, but also that they displayed a cultural holism by employing the same cultural categories as found in other spheres. One illustration from the text will exemplify the point. The first step for a builder is to classify the soil, and soils are classified into four groups: Brahmin soil which is white in colour, Kshatriya soil which is blood red, Vaisya soil which is yellow, and Sudra soil which is black. The text then says if a man lives on the soil of his own caste, he will be happy. But a Brahmin can live on any one of the four classes of soils, a Kshatriya can live on three, a Vaisya on two, and a Sudra on only that which belongs to his caste. 'If, through temptation, a man lives on soil which belongs to a caste higher than his own, then surely destruction shall follow him. The place where his house stands shall be converted into a waste and jackals shall fill the place with their cries even during the daytime' (Bose 1932: 12–13). He used the insights gained from these texts and his own study of Oriya temples to formulate his theories of Indian civilisation. In *Konaraker Bibaran*, Bose (1960a [1926]) refers to an expansive and confident phase of Indian civilisation. In a larger perspective, he considered Oriya civilisation no different from other civilisations in being made up of elements derived from many tribes and many lands. He illustrates this through the sculptures on temple walls.

Bose took up the problems of dating Indian temples in his presidential address to the Anthropology and Archaeology Section of the Indian Science Congress in 1949 (Bose 1967: 85–104). He suggested that archaeology could benefit from anthropology because anthropology also sought to arrange a huge mass of undated facts in proper order. Initially, from the time of Tylor, evolutionary theory was employed for this purpose, but it failed to devise any means of verifying its findings with the help of independent evidence. This theory was rejected by the 'Historical School of America, led by Boas, Wissler, Lowie, Goldenweiser and Kroeber', and it was later replaced on the Continent by what was termed the 'Cultural Historical Method in Ethnology' (*ibid.*: 85). Bose then points out:

> Kroeber not only applied the Diffusion Method with great skill in unravelling the history of a primitive religion in aboriginal America, but also tried to corroborate the findings by means of independent evidence obtained

> from excavation. It is the purpose of the present paper to suggest a similar procedure with regard to the problem of dating ... The particular field of culture from which data will be drawn will be that of Indian architecture, and we can thus hope that workers in both archaeology and anthropology can co-operate with chances of being of real service to one another. (Bose 1967: 85)

Taking his cue from anthropological research, Bose was critical of early historians who depended primarily on a unilinear theory of evolution for dating temples and therefore lacked adequate means for checking their results. He pointed out that the anthropological evidence suggests that different elements of culture do not follow the same rate of diffusion—'They, in fact, display different ranges of variability at the same point of time, and also variable rates of differentiation and of secondary elaboration in course of time' (Bose 1967: 96). He argued that in temples, ornamental elements may have followed one line of evolution, for instance, while structural elements like the height, curvature, or techniques of balancing the weight of the structure, may all have followed completely different rates of change. He did not rule out the contribution of personal genius, which may have been responsible for certain modifications.

Bose argued that if structural elements were not taken into account for the preparation of the scale, then an injustice would be done to the very object of the study. He therefore first considered the space variations suggested by Fergusson (1808–1883), who was considered an authority on Indian architecture, especially temple architecture, and then employed the Distribution Method for rearranging the elements in a time scale.

Bose maintained that a proper scientific method of dating would require employing a uniform method to analyse the structural elements for all temples. After collection of sufficient data, distribution maps of significant elements should be prepared to draw inferences about the course of evolution. He pointed out, however, that the evolutionary scale thus constructed for one state may have limited value in another; hence, in each state the dated temple should be employed to build up another local series. This would be a device to check the findings of the distribution method and, if necessary, to supplement it in the local context: 'By this effort we should also be able to raise our science to higher levels of reliability' (Bose 1967: 104).

The principal relationship between anthropology and archaeology was mediated and constituted by the paradigm of science. Bose was not particularly interested in prehistoric archaeology, but rather in the traditions of classical archaeology and its relation to the study of civilisations. Through his study of temple architecture, he attempted to demonstrate the multiple links between anthropology and archaeology, both in theory and method, in order to evolve a scientific practice distinct from the received traditions of the West. As with his essays on other subjects, in this particular case also, Bose framed his methodology on the basis of extensive observation and detailed knowledge. This is reflected in another of his consistent and enduring concerns, namely, the analysis of the castes and tribes of India.

Structure of Castes and Tribes

In one of his Bengali essays published in 1935 and entitled '*Bharate Nritattvacharchar Ekti Adhyay*' (A Chapter in the Anthropology of India), Bose traced the history of research on the castes and tribes of India. He pointed out that in the early phase the tendency was to construct ethnography for India as a whole. When this was found inadequate, ethnographers concentrated on individual provinces, and it was only when even this was found deficient that the focus shifted to the study of individual castes and tribes (Bose 1935: 63–65). Bose concluded his essay by stating that proper ethnography for the whole of India would require the meticulous collection of information for about twenty years through the collective efforts of various institutes and universities. A quarter century later, while writing a foreword to the book *Data on Caste in Orissa*, published by the Anthropological Survey of India (of which he was then the director), Bose wrote:

> It is the purpose of the present series, entitled Data on Caste, to supplement the current information on changes in rank as ascertained by changes in interaction by an examination of castes' own mechanism for the regulation of internal and external affairs. Data alone are presented from Orissa. These will be followed by other data from Bengal, Madras, etc. On the whole, no generalisation will be attempted; for that can profitably be undertaken when comparative material has been accumulated from all parts of India. (Bose 1960b: vii)

Though the project was never completed, the statement shows Bose's keenness to collect detailed and comprehensive information on the castes (and tribes) of India and his conviction that only once this was done could any theoretical proposition be attempted.

Nevertheless, Bose did have some definite ideas on caste in India. Caste, he believed, was mainly governed by the principles of economic organisation: 'just as capitalism is one way of organising production, caste in India is another way of organising production and distribution' (Bose 1960b: v). However, there were certain important differences as well, for instance, entry into the profession was hereditary in the caste system; caste denied freedom of enterprise; and as a system it was interlaced by reciprocal ties of duties and obligations. According to Bose, the persistence of the caste system could be attributed to the economic and cultural security provided by the non-competitive, hereditary, vocation-based productive organisation which operated in self-sufficient village communities. He did not, however, present caste in idyllic terms, pointing out the unjustifiable legal discrimination against the *sudras* and their economic exploitation within caste society. While caste assured employment and security, it simultaneously preserved the dominance of privileged groups, and this prevented the full and unhampered growth of those who ranked low in the hierarchy.

An interesting feature of Bose's account of caste is the way he located the system within the overall cultural and civilisational norms of Hindu society. He attempted to show that though there was restricted economic freedom under caste, there was a very large measure of cultural freedom. Cultural freedom arose out of the Hindu belief that 'each culture is suited to the particular people who profess it' (Bose 1967: 223). Bose related this attitude to the idea of the freedom of the individual, which, according to him, was held to be the supreme good. Cultural freedom ensured in many ways the growth of the individual to the fullest potential without impediment. Bose thus characterised the Indian respect for cultural autonomy in terms of Gandhi's dictum that 'there are as many religions as there are individuals.' Anticipating Louis Dumont's interpretation of renunciation, Bose argued that regimentation was necessary for the sake of collective economic and social welfare, but that simultaneously arrangements were made for releasing the individual from all forms of social obligation if he so desired.

> Thus, although, Hindu society suppressed the individual under normal conditions, yet the restriction took on a voluntary character, as he could escape from its rigours through the backdoors of the institution of *sannyasa*... And thus, in a way, this special arrangement for safeguarding the individual's freedom acted like compensation against the totalitarian character of the system of caste: Each helped to render the other more stable and permanent. (Bose 1967: 225)

Dumont, in exactly similar fashion, called this renouncer an 'individual-outside-the-world' who leaves his social role in order to adopt a role that is both universal and personal (Dumont 1970 [1966]: 184–188). Society and the renouncer thus made a whole, consisting of two different things, namely, a world of strict interdependence where the individual had no place, and an institution which transcended interdependence by inaugurating the individual.

A firm believer in pluralism, Bose regarded certain elements in India's social culture as contributing permanently to human civilisation, for instance, the democracy of cultures, and 'the safety valve which India created in the form of *sannyasa*', by providing the individual with an option 'when the authoritarian character of the social structure proved too oppressive for him personally' (Bose 1967: 233). In the last part of his Bengali book *Hindu Samajer Garan*, Bose showed how the structure of Hindu society, which remained unaltered during several centuries of Muslim rule, was transformed by colonialism. He explained the stability of Hindu society with reference to its basic design, wherein castes remained integrated by the provisions of economic security and cultural autonomy: 'The stability of Indian civilisation was made possible only by the stability of the economic centre of gravity of the caste system. It is most important to understand this fundamental truth' (Bose 1975 [1949]: 167). This productive system was thrown into disorder, according to Bose, by the onslaught of colonialism. In the economic field, caste was seriously weakened by the intrusion of a system of production and economic relations which was foreign to it. Bose believed that, in the final analysis, the caste system was a judicious combination of social interdependence—the idea that man was subservient to society alongside a catering to the needs of the individual. While accepting that Western capitalism released economic energies among a people, Bose cautioned his readers about the damage capitalism had caused through an excess of individualism. He believed society needed a proper combination of rights and obligations, and in this there was still something to be learnt from the caste system. In the concluding pages of *Hindu Samajer Garan*, Bose writes:

> When we encounter what is offensive in the traditional caste system, we should not spare it. But if we find something valuable in the ancient system of production and of social solidarity, or of regulating the relationship between man and society, something which we may be able to put to use, we should certainly accept it. (Bose 1975 [1949]: 170)

Bose pursued the same argument in relation to tribes and their relationship to Hindu society, claiming that just as Hindu civilisation had recognised *jati* (caste), it had also recognised *jana* (tribe), and that both had coexisted in India for several millennia. Continuing with his logic that Hindu society provided both economic security and cultural autonomy to various groups, Bose argued for the recognition of a special kind of acculturation process, which he called the Hindu method of tribal absorption. The distinctiveness of this method was that it accommodated tribals within the Hindu fold without requiring them to abandon their cultural practices. Béteille quite rightly points out that Bose believed that the two modes of social organisation, which may loosely be described as the 'Brahminical' and the 'tribal', had coexisted in India for a very long time (Béteille 1975: 5–6). The first mode was more complex, much larger in scale, and had a technological base superior to the second. Marginal communities were attracted to Brahminical civilisation not because of its political power but for its technical efficiency and the rights that these communities enjoyed to practise their distinctive customs even when they were arranged in a hierarchy. In *Hindu Samajer Garan* (1975 [1949]) Bose demonstrated, through his analysis of various types of oil presses in India, how the technology of oil presses was associated with caste ranking and inter-caste relationships.

He argued that Hindu society had built up a social organisation on the basis of hereditary, monopolistic, non-competitive guilds and guaranteed monopoly in particular occupations to tribals who came within its fold. He illustrated this with the example of the Juangs of Pal Lahara. The Juangs, who at one time had lived by hunting and collecting, gradually shifted to bamboo-based crafts and earned their living by selling articles to neighbouring people:

> Thus, instead of being economically more or less self-contained, they have now been tagged on to the larger body of Hindu society; they now form only one cog in the wheel of the advanced productive machinery of the Hindus. In the matter of this manufacture of bamboo articles, the Juangs enjoy virtual monopoly in the state of Pal Lahara, and no other caste would willingly engage in that manufacture for fear of losing its own social position. (Bose 1967: 204–205)

The history of acculturation, according to Bose, followed the model of 'sanskritisation' and in the process tribes emerged as castes or subcastes. This particular strategy of tribal absorption had two major implications for Indian society. First, the accommodation of impoverished tribals within the fold of the more successful productive organisation of Hindus had been easy; and second, this prevented the possibility of revolt by the tribes despite their being relegated to a lowly position within Hindu society. Bose concluded his analysis of the Hindu mode of acculturation by observing that economic relations played a crucial role in the sphere of social and cultural relations as culture flowed from a politically and economically dominant group to a subservient one:

> From this, we may venture to suggest with regard to current problems in our national life, that if we wish to set the Juang, the Munda or the so-called untouchable castes on an equal footing with ourselves in a democratically organised society, we should make sure of economic reorganisation first if we want to build the new social order on a permanent basis. (Bose 1967: 215)

Man and Development

Both as a professional anthropologist and later as Commissioner for Scheduled Castes and Scheduled Tribes, Bose deliberated quite intensely on the question of the welfare of tribals and lower castes: The 'General Review' sections of the Report by the Commissioner bear testimony to Bose's dedication. One can detect in these reviews the imprint of a nationalist social thinker, a Gandhian deeply sympathetic to the 'weakest among the weak' (Bose 1972).

In the Hindu mode of acculturation, when a tribe passed from its independent status to membership within the caste system, this transference, according to Bose, was merely from one form of 'totalitarian culture' to another. He associated the process of tribal disintegration in his times with the growth of individualism under the new economic dispensation. 'The chief point to which attention is being drawn', he writes, 'is that individualism in an exaggerated form is responsible for a rapid disintegration of tribal cultures in a way ... which [had] never before occurred in the history of India's cultural evolution' (Bose 1972: 51). He advocated toning down this enthusiasm for individualism and its substitution by a new sense of social cooperativeness in an enlarged sphere to arrest the 'corrosive action' to which tribal cultures had been subjected. Bose's prescription for the development of the tribals and lower castes basically consisted of finding ways to integrate them within the modern economic structure so that caste-based occupational specialisations were eliminated. In the General Review Section he writes:

> Although a very large proportion of the scheduled castes and scheduled tribes are now engaged in agriculture, it is necessary either to take some of them to workshops, or to bring various forms of industries into the villages which can be practised by artisans, or farming families in their spare time. ... as far as practicable, scheduled castes in particular should be taken away from caste-based occupations to those which have no association with caste. This will, at least, loosen the ranking system which holds in the case of caste based industries in rural India. (Bose 1972: 166)

Bose thus preferred a path of development that would eventually avoid the pitfalls of individualism engendered by economic modernisation and the vices of hierarchy in Indian society.

In his plans for action Bose repeatedly emphasised the need for better education, health, hygiene, sanitation, and consciousness of their rights among scheduled tribes and scheduled castes. These actions, however, would have to be initiated by the state, and in Bose's thinking the state and the national political structure appear as basically benevolent, devoted to the minimisation of clashes of values between different cultural elements and to the creation of a more positive relationship between the 'underdeveloped' and the 'developed'. Bose was an active participant in Gandhian politics and, as a student of Indian society, not unaware of unequal power relations within society. However, being a cultural anthropologist and focusing on cultural differences, he often tended to obscure the fact that it is the structures of social and politico-economic dominance which create development problems.

If one adopts a deconstructionist approach to Bose's ideas about development, one notices that certain key constructs he used, namely equality, participation, needs, restructuring of rural social relations, poverty, etc., originated in the West, being later used and transformed in Third World development discourse. Contemporary development theory has exposed the arbitrary character of these concepts, their cultural and historical specificities, and the dangers that their use represents in the context of the Third World. Bose's anthropology also overlooked the ways in which development operated as an arena of cultural contestation and identity construction. Though his ideas about welfare and development were Gandhian, the scientist in him also believed in certain modernist concepts which he thought had universal application. A sympathetic examination of Bose's anthropology, however, leads to the realisation that Bose was sensitive towards the idea of culture as interactive and historical, even though he was unable to work out the full implications of his conceptual scheme. One can detect in these accounts the imprint of a nationalist social thinker, a Gandhian deeply sympathetic to the 'weakest among the weak'. Bose believed that tribal disintegration in his times was associated with the unbridled growth of individualism under the new economic dispensation. Bose's prescription for the development of tribals and lower castes basically consisted of finding ways to integrate them within the modern economic structure so that caste-based occupational specialisations were eliminated. Bose thus preferred a path of development that would eventually avoid the pitfalls of individualism engendered by economic modernisation and vices of hierarchy in Indian society. Bose believed in anthropological intervention for the cause of 'development'; however, contemporary thinking suggests that all anthropological interventions are based on ideological and political criteria. Bose's strategy of intervention reflects an ideology which views the state as benevolent and welfare programmes as paternalistic extensions of a benevolent state.

For the proper welfare of tribals, he advocated an objective, impartial, and scientific assessment of the actual state of affairs as the first necessity. In his essay on anthropology and tribal welfare, Bose began by noting that anthropology was not 'a science of curiosities', and in a place like India where a vast amount of work in the field of tribal welfare remained to be done, 'one must make a special endeavour [to prevent] the science from being misshapen either by the spirit of curio-hunting or by an unbalanced, romantic concern for the hitherto neglected tribes inhabiting our land' (Bose 1967: 191). He warned that if anthropologists failed to do this, 'there is a likelihood of social anthropology being distorted by our inner sympathies' (*ibid.*: 197), a failure to fulfil its duties and responsibilities. In working for the tribals 'we must be extremely cautious not to encourage separatist tendencies, and thus ultimately defeat the very purpose of an all-round freedom, such as the Government of India have resolved to attain' (*ibid.*). Contemporary thinking in theoretical anthropology suggests that all anthropological intervention is based implicitly or explicitly on ideological and political criteria. Bose's strategy of intervention, as mentioned, reflects an ideology which views the state as benevolent and welfare programmes as paternalistic extensions of a benevolent state. Consequently, applied anthropology as imagined by Bose lacks sensitivity both to the political implications of the discipline and to the possible conflicts of interest which may become focused upon an anthropological intervention.

In fact, even during Bose's lifetime the scientific anthropology that he represented and which presumed the ethnographer's transcendental right to cultural objectification were being called into question, not because the tribes were dying out but because they were increasingly becoming subjects of their own history and readers of their own ethnographies. The epistemological illusions on which classical anthropology was based, and the claims to scientific transparency (fieldwork as a simple device for recording pre-existing social data), had begun to wear. As current research shows, governmental intervention in social restructuring and cultural reconstruction, advocated by anthropologists earlier in the name of development, often resulted in subversive social and symbolic micro-processes of 'resistant adaptation'.

Nation-Building and Nationalist Discourse

As an active member and observer of the nationalist movement, Bose believed in India as a unifying idea and concept. In an essay on the problems of Indian nationalism, he began by observing:

> Today, India is passing through a period of great strain, and there are some people who see in it the signs of complete political dismemberment of the country in future. There is one school of thought which emphasises the view that India was never a single country in the past. When others talk about the cultural unity of India, this school ridicules the idea, and says that such unity lies only in the fond imagination of nationalistically minded sentimentalists. Personally, I do not share the pessimism of this school. (Bose 1969: 1)

He considered the question of national unity at three levels—the political, the economic, and the cultural—and argued that it was the economic structure, governed by the organisation of caste, that had brought about 'uniformity' in India's economic structure. As discussed earlier, Bose viewed caste as a system which reduces conflict and competition and guides economic life by a 'moral code' in which sectional demands are subordinated to the welfare of the local community. The strength of the caste system, according to Bose, was that the unit of inter-caste co-operation could be reduced to a very small territorial dimension in case of an emergency, and that was how the system had endured even during periods of acute political disturbance.

This was a typical, and enormously influential, nationalist argument—which considered caste an essential element of Indian society and which distinguished caste as an empirical-historical reality from the ideal of caste. In this context Partha Chatterjee points out:

> Gandhi used to argue that the empirical reality of caste discrimination and even its sanction in the religious texts had "nothing to do with religion". The ideal fourfold *varna* scheme ... did not imply a hierarchy of privilege. ... Since then, successive generations of Indian sociologists, working with increasingly detailed and sophisticated ethnographic materials, have propounded the idea that there is a systematic form to the institutionalised practices of caste, that this system is in some sense fundamental to a characterisation of Indian society, and that it represents a way of reconciling differences within a harmonious unity of the social order. (Chatterjee 1995: 174)

At the political level, Bose had no doubt that India had been successful in creating an integrated nation-state thanks to the British legacy of administration. But, in spite of a common political structure, Bose was seriously concerned about the development of sectional interests putting an enormous strain on national unity. For him, the real issue was to promote integration at the economic level, which he felt had suffered corrosion with the dismantling of the caste system. The promotion of cultural unity was not so important because traditionally India had always encouraged cultural diversity so long as people strictly followed the economic organisation of caste and more or less conformed to the Brahminical code of laws and morals. '*Lokachara, desachara* and *kulachara* were preserved, encouraged and even honoured' (Bose 1969: 6). That is why he was opposed to the propagation of a national language for the whole of India as a solution to the threat of disintegration: 'This seems to be like covering by means of a clean white shroud the body of a dangerously sick patient which is full of festering sores. Such a belief in the magical powers of linguistic unity is unfortunately not likely to lead us very far in the solution of problems which our nationalism is facing today' (*ibid.*). He advocated objective historical analysis in some detail to diagnose the problem. In his historical analysis of social and economic disintegration, Bose observed that social change had been unequal in the various parts of India. A growing population, rising expectations, and limited resources had exacerbated this inequality and produced new problems. One such problem, according to Bose, was Hindu-Muslim relations. He points out that, historically, both Hindu and Muslim upper or middle classes had kept away from the political movements of peasants and the tribes and were unable to reap any political benefit out of these:

> The educated Hindu ... progressively became secularised as he tried to reform Hindu society, as in Bengal, by a re-orientation of his beliefs so as to render him fit to participate in the new order. In contrast the Moslems shed their "contamination", accepted Western education only at its worldly level, and hardly permitted it to operate at the social and cultural levels, and tried to become more firmly entrenched in Islam. In other words, the Moslem became more Moslem, while the Hindu became less of a Hindu in so far as orthodoxy in rituals was concerned; and thus the distance between the two went on increasing. (Bose 1969: 17)

Bose dwelt at considerable length on the history of numerous attempted solutions to the Hindu-Muslim problem, and on how political leaders failed to realise that appeasement alone would not be able to bring about a satisfactory solution to a vexed issue. He argued that, in addition to the communal problem, which was primarily related to the question of Muslim identity and backwardness, a new notion of backwardness had emerged in pre-independent India, based upon language and birth. This he characterised as basically communal in nature:

> Ever since that fateful day (in 1939) when the Working Committee decided that representation in legislatures and services should be in proportion to the population of various "communities", India has been led by progressive steps into the dreary sands of provincialism, linguism and casteism. ... it all began with the communal representation of the Moslems, when representation on a territorial or functional basis gave way to communal considerations. ... one political step which could have brought about a deeper sense of national integration was progressively replaced by another which led more and more towards weakening of the bonds of nationalism. (Bose 1969: 34)

According to Bose, the political leadership did not properly counteract these separatist tendencies in the post-Independence era. He argued for the promotion of associations based on the unities of territorial, economic, civic, and cultural interest rather than caste, language, and religious identities. In other words, he believed that the social base for reforms in democratic participation had been weak to begin with. Adult franchise, which he thought of as a reform of the right kind, coupled, however, with concessions made to communities, had led to sharpened cleavages rather than to the promotion of national solidarity.

The leading ideas of the nationalist elites at Independence can be summarised in terms of sovereignty, unity, order, secularism, democracy, economic self-sufficiency, and the need for social and cultural reforms. However, Bose believed that there was a massive contradiction between the rhetoric of Indian public discourse and the reality of political practice. Indeed, he did not conceal his antipathy for every kind of divisiveness promoted by political practice, advocating instead the development of civil-social associations based on secular identities:

> One argument in favour of separatist patronage lies in the claim that the more neglected communities have to be specially looked after in order to save them from exploitation. Our contention however is that each community in India is divided into exploiters and exploited.... If exploitation has to be ended, which is one of the objectives set forth in our Constitution, then it would be far more desirable for all those who live within a limited territory to become combined into one for its eradication. Any sectional treatment of the disease of exploitation is likely to encourage communal separatism rather than serve the interest of national unity. (Bose 1969: 35)

This overriding concern for 'national unity' in Bose's writing reproduces the nationalist discourse of unified India, in the process neglecting the views of those situated at different locations in Indian society, who have their own distinctive conceptions of the nation. The introduction of democracy in a developing country is not a 'solution' to growing power conflicts; rather, demands for more control and power by various identities are characteristic of multicultural democracies, especially developing-country democracies. Bose's solution to the vexed problem of nation-building argues for unity in the economic domain and pluralism in the cultural sphere, though the cultural conditions prevailing in developing countries (local identities and attachments, hierarchical authority structure, prevalence of community norms, etc.) often forge new identities which, though identified as 'non-national', have nevertheless been able to challenge the dominant discourse.

Metropolis and Social Order

The major cities of post-colonial India are either directly creatures of colonialism or have emerged in response to it. While cities enabled more regular contacts between elites and allowed individuals to conceive of themselves as members of a single, large community, the enumeration and classification of individuals into categories of caste and religion and the introduction of electorates divided along communal lines simultaneously solidified exclusionary identities. In the West, the city was a domain of freedom which liberated the individual from traditional ties; colonial cities, however, reinforced contrary tendencies in Indian society. Bose conducted a social survey in 1962 to investigate selected aspects of social life in Calcutta: for instance, the distribution of linguistic groups, voluntary institutions, occupations, religious divisions, and so on (Bose 1968). He characterised Calcutta as a 'premature metropolis' and summed up his findings thus:

> Calcutta today is far from being a melting pot on the model of cities in the US. In Calcutta the economy is an economy of scarcity. Because there are not enough jobs to go around, everyone clings as closely as possible to the occupations with which his ethnic group is identified and relies for economic support on those who speak his

> language, on his co-religionists, on members of his own caste and on fellow immigrants from the village or district from which he has come. By a backwash, reliance on earlier modes of group identification reinforces and perpetuates differences between ethnic groups. (Bose 1965: 102)

One of the subjects of Bose's investigation was the working of voluntary institutions belonging to various linguistic groups. Bose pointed out that these voluntary institutions were mostly community based, and there were only a few in which several communities could meet to satisfy their common civic or cultural needs. In this context he made some interesting observations on Bengali networking, observing that Bengalis had a strong sense of what he called 'local patriotism'. The range of their social networking was also small, culminating in the building up of a library, a club, or a sports or social service organisation. Since these formations did not have any deeper ideology they tended to split when differences arose: 'A Bengali seems to feel happier in the company of those with whom he closely agrees, rather than in the company of others with whom he may have points of difference. Unities are not stressed; differences are not easily tolerated. This subjects some institutions to repeated forces of fission' (Bose 1968: 79).

Bose noted that even though communities may have lived in a neighbourhood for a considerable length of time, separateness persisted, and he attributed the causes of such exclusive identities to the lack of cultural overlap, and to the inability of classes to abolish linguistic and regional ties or obliterate cultural differences. In moments of crisis, he observed, class unities did not hold and communities fell back upon their regional, linguistic, or religious identities.

Immigrants, according to Bose, tended to re-create their local, cultural and social environment in the city. Thus, in the city of Calcutta there was a situation of cultural pluralism, with different linguistic and regional immigrant communities living in their own cultural worlds. In this context, voluntary institutions acted as adaptive mechanisms and helped create a familiar environment in an alien or strange urban situation by assuming cultural and welfare functions. Due to restricted job opportunities in Calcutta, there was little labour mobility, ensuring that a job seeker would rely on his community ties for a placement rather than compete in the open market:

> Thus social identities which ought to have dissolved if employment opportunities had been constantly on the increase became reaffirmed. This was basically not the fault of the Indian social system, but the fault of a native capitalism which tried to thrive under the shadow of a colonial economy. It drove men into retaining even in the city some of the features of their small scale rural culture. (Bose 1968: 83)

Of course, it has been argued by some that Indian cities and villages are governed by the same structural features of caste and kinship, and are parts of the same civilisation (Pocock 1960: 63–81). Thus, if caste and kinship are considered primary in society, their presence in the city is no more surprising than elsewhere. Over-hasty correlation of urban with Western values and influences seems untenable.

One of Bose's recurring interests was the future of caste in India in the context of occupational change. In *Hindu Samajer Garan* he dwelt at length on census figures to assess the relationship between caste and occupational change; for Orissa he did a similar exercise (discussed above), and for Bengal he compiled data from various regions of Bengal in 1942 in a book entitled *Biallisher Bangla* ('Bengal of 1942', Bose 1971). For the city of Calcutta, too, he investigated the structure and organisation of caste among its residents, concluding: 'There is something like caste in the residential concentration of language groups as well as in their preference for particular ways of making a living. In spite of [the] growth of classes, Calcutta has thus developed a kind of rural arrangement which is strongly reminiscent of caste in the villages' (Bose 1968: 83).

Bose related this city structure to another of his favourite themes, namely, cultural pluralism. As discussed, caste according to Bose had traditionally encouraged pluralism. He pointed out that this superstructure of cultural pluralism had persisted in the civic community of Calcutta and helped indirectly in maintaining communal differences: precisely for this reason, he characterised the city as an imperfect metropolis.

We must remember that colonial cities like Calcutta and Bombay were different from the traditional cities of India and discontinuous with India's own rich urban life. They were imperfect to begin with, the colonial power administering the public space in accordance with its alien concepts, creating cities more as showpieces designed to display the superior rationality and power of the colonial state apparatus, but rendering them deficient in productive capacities. The grandeur of the colonial city remained external to the life of local society. In other words, the contrary tendencies that Bose portrayed in his study of Calcutta were reinforced by colonial policies, and, instead of free individuals, caste and religious groups began to emerge as collective actors in the city. Bose assumed the model of the Western city as his desired model for Calcutta, and when he characterised Calcutta as an imperfect metropolis he did not conceal his expectations for the city in terms of Western standards. What he discounted in the process was the distorted origins of the colonial city and the specificities of the colonial imagination associated with it.

Vernacularisation of Anthropology

Bose, who always called himself a scientist, said science was his *swadharma*. He had a firm faith in the efficacy of scientific research, not simply for the discovery of truth but also towards formulating correct social policies. He conceived of anthropology as primarily a field science: the training of an anthropologist as a scientist was accomplished in the field. He was not particularly interested in developing any abstract conception of science but believed in the efficacy of science through practice. As Béteille points out,

> Bose was well aware that the scientific tools with which he worked were rough-hewn and homemade, and he was perhaps a little proud of this. In all matters he sought to be self-reliant and he felt that if he spent all his energies

> in the endless refinement of his scientific tools, the wider purpose of his enquiry will be defeated. (Béteille 1975: 16)

In the true spirit of an empiricist, he considered himself a field scientist and believed that simple scientific truths could be elicited from the empirical world. For Bose, this science was objective, based on a disinterested analysis of 'facts'. Knowledge consisted of the marshalling of facts, their objective analysis and presentation. He regarded fieldwork-based accounts of caste, tribe, etc., as contributing to the accumulation and expansion of factual (read true) knowledge about India.

It is well known that Bose was an indefatigable fieldworker; he called himself a *paribrajak*, a wanderer, and like a medieval wanderer he was always attempting to discover and propagate truth. He wrote extensively in Bengali to propagate the truth, explaining Indian society and history to non-professionals. In this, he was following the nineteenth-century Bengali tradition of making knowledge available in the vernacular to a non-specialist, non-academic but interested public, an outlook that emerged partly in response to the so-called colonial modernity. Many societies for the 'acquisition of knowledge' were founded in the nineteenth century, and members of these societies discussed and published in Bengali what they thought of as useful knowledge. Rajendralal Mitra (1822–1891), in his journal *Bibhidhartha Sangraha* (1862–1874), regularly published short pieces containing descriptions of ethnic communities in India and abroad, e.g., the Todas, Santals, Tibetans, Kukis, Australian aborigines, and Polynesians, their marriage rites, customs, manners and so on (Bose 1998). Like his predecessors, Bose believed that the fruits of knowledge should be made widely available and not restricted within narrow professional confines.

Bose had no confusion about the public role of both the discipline and its practitioners. He inherited an intellectual tradition which tried to combine professional pursuits with active involvement in the process of national transformation. He was an indefatigable fieldworker partly because of his training, but also because of his Gandhian convictions, which made him believe that ideas were nothing if they were not tested through experience. As a professional he believed that his public role required him to build and develop indigenous institutions, and thus he hardly published anything abroad. Even in India, besides those in professional journals, many of his writings were published in popular and semi-popular periodicals in English and Bengali. His most influential work *Hindu Samajer Garan* (Bose 1975 [1949]) was first published in serial form in the popular Bengali literary magazine *Desh*.

While recent anthropological critiques have pointed to the use of various literary tropes to frame facts culled from the field even in so-called scientific ethnographies, in vernacular anthropology this is a self-conscious part of ethnographic practice, designed to produce a text that is attractive and readable for the lay person. Scientific narration or documentation takes a back seat, and the language itself imposes control over the text. After all, as Roland Barthes puts it, the text is always 'held in language', existing 'only as discourse' (Barthes 1977). Many of Bose's ethnographic accounts and fieldwork experiences were written in Bengali as personal accounts. They are not considered 'social science' in terms of formal disciplinary norms and are often mistakenly seen as trivial and inconsequential. However, these self-reflexive personal accounts subvert the paradigm of anthropological science. As Pratt points out:

> Even in the absence of a separate autobiographical volume, personal narrative is a conventional component of ethnographies. It turns up almost invariably in introduction or first chapters, where operating narratives commonly recount the writer's arrival at the field site, for instance, the initial reception by the inhabitants, the slow, agonising process of learning the language and overcoming rejection, the anguish and loss at leaving. Though they exist on the margins of the formal ethnographic description, these conventional opening narratives are not trivial. They play the crucial role of anchoring that description in the intense and authority-giving personal experience of field work. (Pratt 1986: 31–32)

Bose often made this shift to personal narrative, especially but not exclusively in his Bengali writing. In an essay on the planning of a field investigation, Bose points to the distinction between a traveller's account and proper scientific observation: 'A traveller may, of course, gather a large assortment of materials which may, in future, be of service to various classes of scientific men. But planned field investigation is different from a traveller's observation; it is comparable to experimental observation in a laboratory rather than to the varied observations of a naturalist' (Bose 1953 [1929]: 255). However, a clear continuity with travel writing is evident in the opening narrative of *Hindu Samajer Garan*, a popular book in which Bose attempted to provide a scientific analysis of the structure of Hindu society by combining history, Indology and anthropology. He began the book with a personal narrative:

> In early 1928 I spent a few weeks in a village called Kantala, inhabited by Juangs and Savaras, in the state of Pal Lahara. A visit from [the] outside world is generally a cause of alarm among the Juangs. They thought at first that I had come with some sinister intention, perhaps to investigate for the Forest Department of the Government the collections they made surreptitiously of the forest produce. But when I offered worship to the presiding deity of the village and, after sacrificing two cocks, invited all the villagers to a full meal of rice, the Juangs gave up all their hesitation to accept me as a friend. (Bose 1975 [1949]: 32)

The self of the anthropologist is not effaced in this text. The anthropologist is not merely a scientist-observer, but assumes a multifaceted identity, participating, observing, and writing from multiple, constantly shifting positions.

Vernacular anthropology allowed Bose to emerge from the self-imposed restrictions of scientific anthropology. In *Paribrajaker Diary*, Bose (1982 [1940]) presented an anthropology of people, culture, and tradition, but in a style that was personal, autobiographical, confessional, and anecdotal, and which also depicted his own transition and personal growth in the field. By Bose's own standards the essays fail as science, but it is difficult to exclude them from the domain of anthropology. In these essays Bose deplored urban life, celebrated nature, tribal life, the figure of the *sannyasi*, and expressed his personal joys and sorrows, using the Bengali literary style with great felicity.

Conclusion

Nirmal Kumar Bose had a universalist notion of science, believing that anthropology, like other 'scientific' disciplines, must engage in the progressive discovery of more and more objective knowledge. This was a view shared by early anthropologists in India, inscribed in the discursive practices of the discipline, and rooted in the scientific ideology and methodology of empiricism, positivism, and scientism.

In his writings on the anthropological method he repeatedly stressed the necessity for field surveys, for the gradual accumulation of facts, and for rational inferences. From the very beginning, the early Indian anthropologists were aware of a weak information base for any kind of social analysis. G. S. Ghurye, Bose's contemporary at Bombay University (see chapter two of this volume) also stressed the objective and disinterested compilation of facts, and discouraged hasty theorisation. The 'truth' of society was thus linked to the sovereign power of the empirical gaze that turned the obscurity of darkness into light.

The 'facts' on which Bose relied so much were produced by methods that could not be said to be specific to India. They were produced under the Enlightenment rubric of objective and 'value-free' science. This apparently detached epistemology recognised every new addition to knowledge about India as a new scientific discovery whose veracity was attested to by the scientific standards of the day, independent of any subjective will. If we take the study of caste as an example, Bose's insistence on the collection of data on caste had close parallels with the attempts of colonial administrators to represent India. As Bernard Cohn says:

> In the first instance a caste was a "thing", an entity which was concrete and measurable; above all it had definable characteristics—endogamy, commensality rules, fixed occupation, common ritual practices. There were things which supposedly one could find out by sending assistants into the field with a questionnaire and which could be quantified for reports and surveys. ... This way of thinking about a particular caste was useful to the administrator, because it gave the illusion of knowing the people; he did not have to differentiate too much among individual Indians—a man was a Brahmin, and a Brahmin had certain characteristics. (Cohn 1971: 154)

This was the empirical climate in which information and 'facts' about caste developed into knowledge. A new privilege was accorded to observation and classification. The new and detailed 'objective', 'scientific' scheme was prompted not simply by a desire for knowledge but also by a search for new ways of connecting things, both in the social world and in discourse: a way of making history.

At a more concrete level, as we have seen, Bose located caste in the overall framework of the cultural and civilisational norms of Hindu society. In other words, Bose's description of caste was organised and systematised according to certain normative ideals of Hinduism which were typically Brahminical in nature. This particular idealised model of Hinduism was viewed as an 'acculturative model' for other social groups. However, though Bose, at least theoretically, believed in diffusion and acculturation, his views on caste do not imply acculturation, for acculturation implies a two-way process or reciprocity. On the contrary, Bose's depiction of Hinduism describes a process which vertically integrates various groups into a social structure administered and guided by Brahminical ideals and values. The same vision of the absorptive power of Hinduism explains his argument that tribals were successfully assimilated into the Hindu fold (Bose 1967: 203–215). In a way Bose, like early Orientalist writers, projected Indian social history as essentially the history of Hinduism, or of the assimilation of non-Hindu groups into Hindu society.

As noted above, when Bose argued that the caste system in its ideal form sought to harmonise mutually distinct units into a stable and harmonious social order, he was in fact iterating the nationalist assertion that caste in its ideal form was not oppressive, and that it was not inconsistent with the aspirations of individuality (see Chatterjee 1995: 173–199). It is this view of caste and of 'the unity of Indian society' which prompted Bose to rely on the authority of the state to restructure society after Independence. This is a view that not only failed to recognise conflict, oppression, and hegemony, but also underplayed or completely ignored the role of 'non-national' identities situated at different locations in Indian society. This presumption of a single shared sense of India—a unifying idea and concept of the Indian collective subject based on the trope of 'unity in diversity'—has now all but lost credibility.

In his written texts Bose also attempted to demonstrate the unity of various disciplinary perspectives. Though he was never tired of reiterating the importance of scientific investigation, methodology, and analysis for social knowledge, he himself did not particularly follow the more rigorous scientific prescriptions for anthropology that emphasised a limited subject focus, in-depth fieldwork, codified data accumulation, and cautiously restricted inferences. In his writings and analyses Bose preferred the earlier style of classical encyclopaedism, the comparative method, intuitive hypothesising, and generic conceptualising. Thus, in spite of his scientific proclamations, Bose remained a classical scholar searching for interdependence between the various branches of knowledge. For him social analysis remained a comprehensive, totalising activity combining history, anthropology, Indology, sociology, and related subjects. His Bengali essays, which he wrote in a relatively open style, appear almost contemporary in flavour, very similar to the humanistic mode of anthropological writing, resembling literary criticism. In writing these essays Bose perhaps anticipated that openness, rather than scientific closure, would one day become an inevitable feature of the discipline.

FIVE

RAMKRISHNA MUKHERJEE (1919–2016)

Inferring Inductively: Problems and Paradoxes

Inductive-Inferential Method

Beginning from 1975, for more than three decades Ramkrishna Mukherjee was engaged in developing an inductive methodology for social science. Mukherjee conceptualised his methodology by differentiating between inductive-inferential and deductive-positivistic methods of research. On the basis of his preferred methodology Mukherjee then selected certain important themes from Indian sociology, as for instance, social change, social development and nation building, indicating how these could be conceived and developed. Mukherjee's methodological formulation is founded on four questions, which he considers fundamental for a proper appraisal of a phenomenon. These are: What is it? How is it? Why is it? and What will it be? An initial account of his formulation first appeared in his book *Social Indicators* (Mukherjee 1975: 3; see also, Mukherjee 1972) and in greater detail in his subsequent volume *What Will it Be?* (Mukherjee 1979). Since then he continued to reiterate the basic tenets of this method without any major revisions in his subsequent publications (compare the chart in 1979: 14–16; and 1993: 157–159). It was only in his last book (Mukherjee 1993) in this series that he added a fifth question, namely, 'What should it be?' though without much elaboration. He only mentioned that an answer to this question would make the appraisal much more complete. He pointed out that sociologists should also examine how the two questions, 'What will it be?' and 'What should it be?' could be included within the orbit of social sciences rather than leaving *them* to philosophical speculations (Mukherjee 1993: 131).

The term he uses to explain the operation of this method is 'sciencing society' (*ibid.*: 126) and he writes: 'Sciencing is not yet a frequently used expression; however, it aptly captures the pursuit of knowledge in order to systematically comprehend a phenomenon by answering five sequential questions: What is it? How is it? Why is it? What will it be? What should it be?' *(ibid.)*. From the answers to the five types of questions Mukherjee delineates the basic type and orientation of research. According to him the orientation is descriptive and classificatory with reference to the questions, 'What is it?' and 'How is it?' It becomes *explanatory* when the 'Why is it' question is added and *diagnostic* when 'What will it be?' is also addressed.

In the 'explanatory' mode of research, Mukherjee believes, a theory is often used in a 'deductive-positivistic' manner to answer the third question, but the answer is not always unequivocal (Mukherjee 1979: 9; 1993: 150), while in descriptive and classificatory research, theory is of little relevance as the strategy of research is 'fact-finding' and 'interpretation of fact' found with reference to the questions, 'What is it?' and 'How is it?' (1979: 9). While the space-time coordinates of descriptive and explanatory research form a closed circuit, in diagnostic research it is open at one end; that is why in diagnostic research, according to Mukherjee, it is possible to address the 'What will be?' question.

Since diagnostic research is based on an open system (space-time coordinates are free at the contemporary terminal), the usual method of answering the 'Why is it?' question, in terms of explanatory theory or empirically formulated hypothesis, cannot be applied here. As Mukherjee writes:

> It is now necessary to ascertain from the grassroots level the viability, propensity and proliferation of the system of variation in respect of different stimuli so as to predict, probabilistically, the future course of behaviour of the system. The question "why is it" thus assumes a greater significance than for explanatory research ... Also, in order to facilitate the course of diagnosis and answer the question "what will it be" evermore precisely and comprehensively, the alternate hypothesis should be conceived to form an *infinite but enumerable* series and to emerge unrestrictedly from the field of variation dealing with the "open" system. (Mukherjee 1979: 10–11)

In other words, for a given phenomena, researches in explanatory mode will have different theories; however in the diagnostic mode, all these 'theories' will be given the status of 'alternate hypothesis', and all the known and knowable alternate hypotheses would constitute the 'field of variation' of the phenomenon. The efficiency of a particular hypothesis can then be tested on an inductive base in order to evaluate its relative efficiency vis-a-vis other such hypotheses.

For Mukherjee, different explanations about society are dependent on the subjective preference of a scholar who selects from 'infinite and enumerable' information-space some items that he considers meaningful to explain the 'what', 'how' and 'why' of society in some manner. The information-space, according to Mukherjee, is value-free because 'the items of information do not contain any intrinsic value as being wanted by anyone or not, as being desirable or undesirable or irrelevant to any person' (Mukherjee 1989: 231; 1993: 131). Hence by selecting certain items, a scholar makes a primary evaluation of the value-free information space and thus by appropriating certain items of information-space subjectively, he turns that information into data, that is, as possessing a specific meaning.

It is in this manner that all available or possible scholars create 'an infinite but enumerable data space' out of 'the infinite but enumerable information space'. For instance, the 'what' and 'how' questions restrict the quest for information to mere description and only those items are collected and consolidated out of the available information spaces that are considered relevant to the context. In addition to describing a phenomenon, if an explanation is sought, in that case to answer the question about the phenomenon, information necessary in the context of the theory or hypothesis adopted as the yardstick for explanation are collected. In such cases, according to Mukherjee, researchers are concerned with the search of particular set of data in the given context, because as one adopts one or another established theory or previously formulated hypothesis as the yardstick for explanation, corresponding data spaces will, of course, emerge from the same information space. In diagnostic research, focus is on diagnosis and answering the 'what will it be' question of prediction; hence, here different explanations of a phenomenon are arranged in a series of alternate hypotheses, which include not only theories but also tentative hypotheses (Mukherjee 1983: 4–5). In this case search is not for a particular set of data to explain the phenomenon, but to engage in diagnostic investigations on the relative efficiency of these explanations and, therefore, with various ways of constructing data-sets.

For Mukherjee there are two ways in which a theory can be utilised in social research: as a 'yardstick' to explain a phenomenon on a *deductive* base or as an 'alternate hypothesis' to be tested on an *inductive* base in order to appraise its *relative efficiency* vis-a-vis other such hypotheses (Mukherjee 1979: 7). Mukherjee calls the first formulation as the structure-process-structure (SPS) syndrome for the appraisal of social reality, where a social scientist ascribes datum to a specific set of information items and thus deduces the social structure. Mukherjee writes:

> But, then, we are confronted with many formulations of the structure-process-structure (SPS) syndrome for the appraisal of social reality. This is true not only to explain the causality of the present state of society but also to diagnose what the society will be in the near future. The

> point, therefore, is to ascertain that formulation of the SPS syndrome (or a particular combination of some of the available formulations) which reflects reality in the most precise, unequivocal and comprehensive manner. (Mukherjee 1993: 133)

While the method of individual SPS syndrome is 'deductive and positivistic' the method which will be able to infer probabilistically from all the available and possible SPS syndromes 'that SPS syndrome (or a particular combination of several SPS syndromes) which reflect reality the most precisely, unequivocally and comprehensively' (Mukherjee: 1993: 135), must be inductive-inferential. But since this is higher-order systematisation, Mukherjee is in search of a 'yardstick' by which the relative-efficiency of the SPS syndromes should be judged. Mukherjee finds this 'yardstick' in the 'value of life', or what he calls the four cardinal valuations of humankind, as against ordinal valuations of social theories. For him 'survival, security, prosperity and progress are thus the four cardinal values which are encountered by every human in all places, at all times, and with respect to every group of people' (*ibid.*: 136). For Mukherjee the universal validity of the four cardinal values for human existence is beyond question. However, as the cardinal valuation of life often influences the 'ordinal valuation of the SPS syndrome', hence, for Mukherjee, a method should be found to establish on a probability basis the SPS syndrome which is closest to the realisation of the cardinal valuation of human kind. These value spaces can be systematically explored only on an inductive base, though in the ultimate analysis the relationship between the two kinds of valuation, or more generally the relationship between knowledge and reality, according to Mukherjee, will always remain asymptotic, as he states: 'It [knowledge] may very closely explicate reality, but never fully and finally. Therefore, science can evermore reduce the gap between the ordinal valuations and the cardinal valuation of humankind, but can never reduce the gap to zero' (*ibid.*: 139).

In his critical review of Indian sociology, Mukherjee characterises the main body of Indian sociology as being constrained by the theoretical and methodological limitations of a deductivist-positivist nature and argues that the existing level of knowledge can only be raised by adopting the inductive inferential orientation (Mukherjee 1979a: 138–139). He argues that the inductive-inferential method is capable of handling a lot more variation than the deductive method and since this mode of research follows the principle of induction and inference on a probability basis, this method cannot easily be designated as positivist. It is an approach where the procedure rests upon the total social space of the indivisible elements of the properties of the phenomena to be examined from the bottom upwards, and not from top downwards as it is for the prevalent deductive-positivistic method.

Problems of Induction

It is often said the inference from the hypothesis and initial conditions to the prediction is deductive, but the inference in the opposite direction, from the truth of the prediction to the hypothesis is inductive. Inductive inferences do not pretend to establish their results with certainty; instead they confirm them or make them probable. The whole trouble with looking at the matter this way, as Mukherjee does, is that it appears to constitute an automatic transformation of deductive fallacies into correct inductive arguments. When we discover, to our dismay, that our favourite deductive argument is invalid, we simply rescue it by saying that we never intended it to be deductive in the first place, but that it is a valid induction. With reference to this situation, the logician Morris R. Cohen is said to have quipped, 'A logic book is divided into two parts; in the first (on deduction) the fallacies are explained, and in the second (on induction) they are committed' (Salmon 1968: 143). Surely inductive argument, if it plays a central role in scientific method, must have better credentials.

When questions about deductive validity arise, they can usually be resolved in a formal manner by reference to an appropriate logical system. It is an unfortunate fact that far less attention has been paid to the foundational questions that arise in connection with the empirical sciences and their logic. When questions of inductive validity arise, there is no well-established formal discipline to which they can be referred for definitive solution. A number of systems of inductive logic have been proposed, some in greater and some in lesser detail, but none is more than rudimentary, and none is widely accepted as basically correct (Pap 1962). Questions of inductive correctness are more often referred to scientific or philosophical intuitions, and they are notoriously unreliable guides.

Mukherjee's methodology falls into the empiricist tradition in social science, and this chapter might just as well have been titled 'Empiricism and Induction' for it is the empiricists, by and large, who show the greatest (positive) interest in induction. Therefore a brief look at the role of induction in empiricist epistemology is in order and might help to provide a setting for many of the discussions that follow. A cursory survey of the empiricist tradition from Hume to Reichenbach, Feigl, and Salmon clearly reveals the vital role of induction and probability. In fact, with little, if any, distortion, induction might be viewed as the cornerstone of empiricism: it is central to epistemology, to the theory of concept formation, as well as to the justification of all factual knowledge. What is perhaps not so obvious is that such emphasis calls for a comprehensive theory, not merely bits and pieces. This, then is the task confronting the empiricist—to construct a full-fledged system of inductive logic which is consistent (i. e., free of paradoxes and inconsistencies) and reasonably complete (Bose 1986, 1995). The construction of such a system—and hence the viability of empiricism—hinges, in large part, on the solution of the following problems: (1) *Hume's Problem.* What rationally justifies any inference from the observed to the unobserved, the known to the unknown? (Reichenbach 1949; Black 1958; Feigl 1963; Hempel 1966; Salmon 1968); (2) *Hempel's Paradox.* What is confirming evidence (positive instances) for a hypothesis? (Hempel 1945, 1965; Mackie 1963); and (3) *Goodman's New Riddle of Induction.* What hypotheses are confirmed by positive instances? (Leblanc 1963; Hempel 1966). In principle, until these problems are solved, inductive logic remains in a rather low state; and consequently, empiricism takes on the appearance of being quite heavily dependent on wishful thinking or dogma concerning probability and induction.

In contrast to Mukherjee's contention, it should be stressed that inductive inference must not be thought of as an effective method of discovery, which by a mechanical procedure leads from observational data to appropriate hypotheses or theories. This misconception underlies what might be called the narrow inductivist view of social scientific inquiry, a view that is well illustrated by Mukherjee's pronouncement which can be summarised as follows: first, all facts would be observed and recorded *without selection* or *a priori* guess as to their relative importance; second, the observed and recorded facts would be analysed, compared, and classified *without hypothesis* or *postulates* other than those necessarily involved in the logic of thought; third, from this analysis of facts, generalisation would be inductively drawn as to the relations, classificatory or causal, between them; fourth, further inductive research would be undertaken employing inferences from previously established generalisations.

It need hardly be argued in detail that this conception of 'scientific procedure', and of the role induction plays in it, is untenable; the reasons have been set forth by many writers. Let us just note that an inquiry conforming to this idea would never go beyond the first stage, for—presumably to safeguard scientific objectivity—no initial hypotheses about the mutual relevance and interconnections of facts are to be entertained in this stage, and as a result, there would be no criteria for the selection of the facts to be recorded. The initial stage would therefore degenerate into an indiscriminate and interminable gathering of data from an unlimited range of observable facts, and the inquiry would be totally without aim or direction. Similar difficulties would beset the second stage—if it could ever be reached—for the classification or comparison of data again requires criteria. These are normally suggested by hypotheses about the empirical connections between various features of the 'facts' under study. But the conception just cited would prohibit the use of such hypotheses, and the second stage of inquiry as here envisaged would again lack aim and direction.

The celebrated problem of induction, which still lacks any generally accepted solution, includes under a single heading a variety of distinct, if related, problems. These problems may be briefly described as (1) the problem of 'justification', (2) the problem of 'differential appraisal' and, (3) the 'analytical problem'. One can distinguish the three problems as follows:

1. Justification: Why, if at all, is it reasonable to accept the conclusions of certain inductive arguments as true—or at least probably true? Why, if at all, is it reasonable to employ certain rules of inductive inference?
2. Differential appraisal: Why is one inductive conclusion preferable to another as better supported? Why is one rule of inductive inference preferable to another as more reliable or more deserving of rational trust?
3. Analytical problem: What is it that renders some inductive arguments rationally acceptable? What are the criteria for deciding that one rule of inductive inference is superior to another?

While Mukherjee believes that the 'inductive-inferential' method is self-justificatory (because for him it is better than what he calls the 'deductive-positivistic' method) he does not really go into the more intricate, foundational, justificatory and analytical problems of induction.

The three problems mentioned above, however, cannot be pursued separately: a comprehensive general defence of inductive procedures involves specification, *inter alia,* of legitimate forms of inductive argument, and selection between alternative inductive rules or methods must rely, explicitly or not, upon determination of what, if anything makes an inductive argument 'sound'. Using Mukherjee's argument a little differently, we can say that the *why* of inductive argument cannot profitably be isolated from the *how*.

Locke once said that induction from experience or empirical investigation 'may provide us convenience, not science'. A demand that induction be justified arises, of course, from supposed deficiency or imperfection; induction always looks inadequate when compared with the supposedly superior certainty of demonstrative reasoning. The nagging conviction that induction somehow falls short of the ideals of rationality perfectly exemplified in valid deductive argument has made the problem of induction needlessly intractable.

The various options suggested in response to Hume's problem can be summarised as follows:

(a) Hume's challenge cannot be met; hence the inductive argument is indefensible, and ought to be expunged from any reasoning purporting to be rational.

(b) In the light of Hume's criticisms, inductive arguments as normally presented need improvement, either i) by adding further premises or, ii) by changing the conclusions into statements of probability, which seems to be Mukherjee's approach. However, in either case a conclusion's validity is expected to follow demonstratively from the premises, and inductive logic will be reconstructed as a branch of applied deductive logic, as we shall see.

(c) The pragmatic option, namely, if induction cannot be validated, it can at least be vindicated.

Probability and Ambiguity

Since Mukherjee's argument derives from the empiricist epistemology where induction is closely associated with enumeration and, therefore, with frequency, he has no alternative but to accept the probabilistic approach to induction, though he does not elaborate his notion of probability. The basic argument in this case is that if there is no prospect of plugging the deductive gap between A and B by adding further premises known to be true, then perhaps the same can be achieved by weakening the conclusion. If B does not follow from A, why not be satisfied with a more modest conclusion of the form 'probably B' or perhaps 'B has such and such a probability relative to A'?

The most rigorous attempt towards arguments of this sort so far available (Keynes, for example) have encountered severe technical difficulties. It is essential to such a programme that the probability of a generalisation relative to an unbroken series of confirmatory instances steadily approach unity. The conditions necessary for this to be possible are at least that the generalisation has an initial non-zero probability and that infinitely many of the confirmatory instances be independent, in the sense of having less than maximal probability of occurrence, given the already accumulated evidence. At this point, those who search for supreme inductive principles find themselves with empty hands. Mill, for instance, relied on 'simple enumeration', defending it on the grounds of universal applicability; Keynes, abandoning his empiricist principle and arguing in the fashion of Kant, suggested that the ultimate principles rest upon 'some direct synthetic knowledge' of the general regularity of the universe. This principle hardly suffices to satisfy these conditions; subsequent criticism has shown that even more rigorous conditions are needed. Some have argued that the desired asymptotic convergence will result only if in the long run every instance of the generalisation is scrutinised – which would certainly render the theory completely useless in practical application. For all his importance as a founder of confirmation theory, Keynes must be judged a failure.

At this point it will not be out of place to mention that though the probability calculus was established early in the seventeenth century, hardly any serious attention was given to the analysis of the meaning of the concept of probability until the latter part of the nineteenth century. Even then, there is no real consensus on this question; there are, instead, three distinct interpretations of the probability concept, each with its own adherents. *A fortiori*, there is no widely accepted answer to the question of the nature of the prior probabilities, for they seem to be especially problematic in character. Among the three leading probability theories, the *logical theory* regards probability as an *a priori* measure that can be assigned to propositions or states of affairs, the *personalistic theory* regards probability as a *subjective measure* of degrees of belief, and the *frequency theory* regards probability as a physical characteristic of types of events.

The logical theory is the direct descendent of the famous classical theory of Laplace. According to the classical theory, probability is the ratio of favourable to equally possible cases. The equi-possibility of cases, which is nothing other than the equal probability of these cases, is determined *a priori* on the basis of a *principle of indifference*, namely, two cases are equally likely if there is no reason to prefer one to the other. This principle gets into deep logical difficulty. This contradiction, known as the Bertrand paradox, brings out the fundamental difficulty with any method of assigning probabilities *a priori*. Such *a priori* decisions have an unavoidable arbitrary component to them, and in this case, the arbitrary component gives rise to two equally reasonable, but incompatible, ways of assigning probabilities.

The personalistic interpretation is the twentieth-century successor of an older and more naive subjective concept. According to the crude subjective view, a probability is no more or less than a subjective degree of belief; it is a measure of our ignorance. Modern personalists do not interpret probabilities as subjective degrees of belief, but rather, as coherent degrees of belief. To say that degrees of belief are coherent means that they are related in such manner as to satisfy the conditions imposed by the mathematical calculus of probability. Personalists interpret degrees of belief that violate the mathematical calculus as analogous to logical inconsistency and recommend some revision or adjustment to bring these degrees into conformity with the mathematical calculus. The chief objection to the personalist view is that it is not objective. Whether and to what extent the lack of objectivity is actually harmful is a different question. Though Mukherjee does not discuss his notion of probability, the interpretation that he implicitly accepts is the frequency theory, the theory that regards a probability as a relative frequency of occurrence in a large sequence of events. It seems evident that there are many contexts where the frequency concept of probability seems well suited to the use of statistical techniques, for example, in quantum mechanics, but it is much more dubious that the frequency interpretation is at all applicable to such matters as the probability of a scientific hypothesis in the light of empirical evidence. In this case where are we to find the large classes and long sequences to which to refer to our probabilities of hypotheses? This difficulty has seemed insuperable to most authors who have dealt with the problem. The general conclusion has been that the frequency interpretation is fine in certain contexts, but we need a radically different probability concept if we are to deal with the probability of hypotheses.

Inductivists prefer the frequency theory, just like Mukherjee, because here probability statements are empirical statements describing the number of times some event has happened relative to the number of times it might have happened (the modem propensity theory of probability is closely related to the frequency theory; Kyburg 1974). For example, if it is observed over the years that a steady 35 per cent of eighteen-year olds in India attend university, then there is a 35 per cent probability of eighteen-year olds in India going to university in the current year. But there are difficulties with the frequency theory when considering unbounded series of events: for example, to avoid being misled by short-run variations, such as the university attendance rate of eighteen-year olds in India during the Second World War, it is necessary to define probability as the limit to which the frequency tends in the long run. Immediately the problem of induction reappears as the problem of trying to estimate the long run or limiting frequency from a finite ran. The uniformity principle has to be invoked: if the future resembles the (recent) past, then there will be a 35 per cent probability of eighteen-year olds in India going to university. Without the uniformity principle, an observed relative frequency in a finite ran is compatible with any limiting frequency, depending on what events happen in the future.

Carnap (1950) after recognising this problem with the frequency theory, turned to an alternative conception of probability in which it is a logical relation between evidence and a conclusion. This view of probability was developed by Carnap

(1954) into confirmation theory, where the aim is to provide the logic of induction, precise rules for calculating the degree of confirmation that a particular set of evidence propositions give a particular conclusion. Despite the sophistication of Carnap's confirmation theory it faces two related difficulties (Bose 1986). First, because a proposition might be confirmed by one set of evidence statement but disconfirmed by other sets, the confirmationist must insist upon the requirement of total evidence before calculating the degree of confirmation of the proposition. Second, Carnap's system of inductive logic assigns a probability of zero to scientific laws formulated as unrestricted generalisations, regardless of the evidence available, since no finite amount of evidence can confirm such generalisation of potentially infinite scope.

Even if modern developments in confirmation theory overcame these difficulties and it became possible to assign a non-zero probability to a law by successfully specifying the degree of confirmation on the basis of all available evidence, this approach to the problem of induction entails modification. A modification has to be made in the deductive-nomological account such that it no longer relies on universal laws but only on probability statements. An appropriately modified scheme called the inductive-statistical explanation has been described by Hempel (1965). However, in Hempel's scheme, probabilistic laws cannot be used to explain or predict the occurrence of singular events. Some authors, persuaded by the difficulties encountered in attempting to justify induction probabilistically, suggest that it is more appropriate to offer a pragmatic justification (Feigl 1952; Salmon 1961). Induction is a rule of the scientific game. Critics of the pragmatic justification of induction argue that it provides no epistemological criteria for discriminating between good and bad inductions. It justifies all inductions equally and hence is no guide for the practice of science, for the choice of laws (Black 1954).

Though Mukherjee illustrates his inductive formulation with appropriate examples, in none of his illustrations is he able to compute the probability of his hypotheses as he cannot effectively demarcate their limits. Hence most of them can be considered as unbounded series. The lack of any probabilistic association of these hypotheses is also significant because, as we have seen, the 'what will be' question is an inalienable part of his theoretical construction.

There is one final related comment to be made upon the frequency theory (the theory that Mukherjee implicitly accepts), although it is a cautionary comment on all the theories of probability. Suppose we consider the probability statement: 'The probability of a sociologist being a philosopher is p.' Although this may give us some degree of numerical confidence, our confidence in the general probability statement itself, as Strawson (1952) and other philosophers point out, is not established thus. For, the latter will depend upon whether the general probability statement is founded upon a sufficient number of well-chosen observations—and this is a matter for the *judgement* so that our reasons for believing a probability statement are not entirely numerical. In other words, the concept of probability is not entirely a matter of numbers.

Inductivism and Positivism

A constant refrain one witnesses in Mukherjee's writing is that the deductive method is positivistic; in fact, he always refers to this form of logic as 'deductive-positivistic', whereas he believes that the inductive method is somehow free from the positivistic trap. That this is a mistaken understanding of positivism we shall see in a moment. But before that some general comments on Mukherjee's views on sociology and social science.

In his understanding of social science Mukherjee shares the positivistic view that phenomena dealt with by the social sciences are qualitatively no different from those of the natural sciences. This being the case, the methodology of the latter is appropriate for the former. The principal aim of sociology for him is to formulate a system of empirically grounded theories that will ultimately be used for accurate prediction of social phenomena (answer to the 'what will be' question). Sociology, for him, has a technical character and the basic thrust of his approach has been towards the production of objective knowledge that is open to quantification (i.e., precise measurement) and demonstrable proof. In fact his favourite citation that appears in many of his writings (1979: 13; 1983: 9; 1989: 30) is from Lord Kelvin reminding everyone that 'when you can measure what you are speaking and express it in numbers, you know something about it, but when you cannot measure it, when you cannot express it in numbers, your knowledge is of a meagre and unsatisfactory kind'. Equating knowledge with measurement is, of course, a very narrow and naive form of positivism, deriving its support from empiricism and scientism, from the belief that social science enquiry would be successful if it were based on objective, value-free measurements and quantification.

Coming back more specifically to the question of inductivism and positivism, we can trace its roots to the Comtean variety of knowledge formation where positivism as a theory of knowledge prescribes that the only kind of sound knowledge available to human kind is that of science grounded in observation. Both inductivism and hypothetico-deductivism amplify the Comtean variety of positivism by describing two different ways in which 'scientific' laws and theories are to be related to experience. Positivism in its inductive form is a theory of 'scientific method' according to which 'science' progresses by inducing laws from observational and experimental evidence (Bose 1995). This is a tradition that goes back to Francis Bacon. As we have discussed, since induction does not justify our accepting the truth of the unrestricted universal laws, this has consequences for the logical-positivists for they require laws for sound explanations; but if laws cannot be conclusively verified by experience then they are metaphysical according to the principle of verifiability. Induction is considered to be in need of justification because it is argued that it is deficient as compared with deduction. In valid deductive inferences, premises conclusively support conclusions (that is, entail them) whereas in inductive inferences they do not. Valid deductions are 'truth-transmitting', whereas sound inductions are only 'likelihood transmitting'.

Related to empiricism and induction there is another conception of positivism in sociology, namely, a theory of knowledge according to which the 'natural science of sociology' consists of the collection and statistical analysis of quantitative data about society. The genealogy of this particular type of positivism can be traced back to Durkheim who added to Comte's abstract philosophical themes another, quite independent tradition, that of statistics. Most notably in his book *Suicide* (1897), he brought together nineteenth-century Comtean social philosophy and the collection and analysis of quantified social facts. This type of positivism is identical with traditional empiricism: positive (as opposed to theological and metaphysical) knowledge is empirical knowledge, which is the only sound (or 'scientific') knowledge because observation (or more generally, experience) is the only sound source of knowledge. This position is opposed to the rationalist one where reason provides indubitable truths about the world, or the dialectical view of knowledge, according to which the only source of sound knowledge is praxis.

A strong positivistic element in Mukherjee's method is due to his inclusion of the 'what will be' question that is, constructing a system in which prediction becomes a necessary component of meaningful social research. This function of prediction evolves out of the positivistic notion of the unity of science and the so-called scientific method. Though it must be said that even if prediction is interpreted probabilistically, probabilistic laws cannot be used to explain or predict a singular state of affairs. Prediction also accepts an unproved assumption about the 'uniformity of nature', which might be more fully stated as 'all uniformities observed hitherto will continue to obtain everywhere and for ever'.

Mukherjee's inductive social science shares all the major elements of positivistic thinking that we have discussed, and he continued to pursue a programme aimed at constructing a natural science of society centering on causal laws derived from or tested by observational data with the aid of statistical techniques, and he is prone to treat the philosophical problems as mere technical difficulties. Among this group of methodological and statistical technicians, doubts about positivist presuppositions in social analysis are assumed to be resolvable by greater attention to the details of data collection and statistical techniques.

Deductive Reconstruction of Inductive Social Science

One of the ironies of Mukherjee's methodological prescriptions is that though he rejects the deductive model as positivistic, inadequate, subjective, and value-loaded (Mukherjee 1993: 131–135), he ultimately takes recourse to the deductive reconstruction of his inductive methodology! This particular defence of induction is not new; some adopted it quite consciously, while others inadvertently fell into this trap.

The effort to provide justification for induction through a reconstruction of inductive arguments so as to make them valid has chiefly taken two forms: a) *search for supreme inductive principles;* and b) *recourse to probability.* In the first case, if, for instance, events occurred purely at random, it would be impossible to make successful inductions; conversely, if inductions of a certain sort do systematically produce true conclusions, there must be a contingent regularity in the universe that should be capable of expression in the form of supreme principles or postulates of induction. Only if such principles/postulates are true can inductions be sound; they must therefore be the assumed but unexpressed premises of all sound inductive arguments.

Favoured candidates for the role of such enabling postulates have been: the principle that the future resembles the past (Hume); a general principle of causation to the effect that every event has a sufficient cause (Mill); a principle of spatio-temporal homogeneity which makes locations and dates causally irrelevant (Mill again); and a principle of limited independent variety ensuring that the attributes of individuals cluster together in a finite number groups (Keynes). Mukherjee introduces his own supreme principles in terms of what he calls 'four cardinal values' which according to him are universally valid. He poses these values as assuming a homogeneity over time and space and asserts that 'survival, security, prosperity and progress are thus the four cardinal values which are encountered by every human in all places, at all times, and with respect to every group of people' (Mukherjee 1993: 136). Any of these supreme principles, if true, records the presence in the universe of a certain global regularity or order which permits inductive procedures to produce the desired true conclusions. In other words, the validity of the inductive method reduces in the end to deductive procedures. One can argue that if supreme premises can be known to be true, the remaining process of inference becomes trivial.

However, there is a serious problem: how can the desired supreme premises ever be known to be true. Since appeal to induction is excluded at this point on the score of circularity, and since the principles themselves cannot be analytic if they are to serve their purpose, there seems no recourse at all. The point simply is, how can Mukherjee show his cardinal principles to be true? At this point those who search for supreme inductive principles find themselves with empty hands. The conclusion seems inescapable that any attempt to show that there are general ontological guarantees for induction is doomed to failure from the outset.

In view of this circularity and empirical falsity of induction, another way of justifying induction by reconstructing it as deduction has been tried. This approach, as we have discussed, instead of bolstering the premises leads to the dilution of the conclusion. It involves converting the conclusion of an inductive inference into a probability statement. Like Mukherjee, this approach still has many adherents. It involves converting the conclusion of an inductive inference into a probability statement. If there is no prospect of plugging the deductive gap between A and B by adding further premises known to be true, then perhaps the same end can be achieved by weakening the conclusion. If B does not follow from A, why not be satisfied with a more modest conclusion of the form 'probably B'?

The extent to which the recourse to probability will accomplish the task will depend upon the interpretation of the concept of probability. With empirical interpretation of probability (e.g., the frequency theory), the probability conclusion covertly refers to finite or infinite sets of events not covered by the given premises. The inductive leap remaining in the reconstructed argument will thus still leave the problem of induction unsolved. If, however, probability is construed in some logical way, the amended conclusion will say less than the premises and will therefore be untouched by subsequent empirical test; the deductive validity of the reconstructed argument will be saved only at the cost of rendering problematic its relevance to prediction and empirical control. In converting a purportedly inductive argument into a valid deductive one, the very point of the original argument—that is, to risk a prediction concerning the yet unknown—seems to be destroyed.

By postulating a supreme principle, or what he calls a cardinal principle and also by arguing for probability, Mukherjee brings back the deductive mode very much into his scheme. In spite of his best efforts and his apparent rejection of the deductivist mode of inference, it creeps in stealthily into his framework and takes over his whole scheme—a fatal flaw that virtually demolishes his edifice.

CONCLUSION

Through the analyses and review of the writings of some early sociologists of India, this book attempts to evaluate the journey of Indian sociology from the perspective of theoretical concerns, methodological and technical choices, and the cognitive and paradigmatic tensions. As Singh rightly observes:

> Sociology in India was in the beginning less professionalized; most of its patrons came from outside this discipline and were not initiated into its logic or methodology. Most of them treated sociology as a style of cultural critique or reformative ratiocination. Its character was thus defined by its responsive yet critical note on the Western interpretations of Indian society, its institutions and cultural pattern. Radhakamal Mukerjee, B. N. Seal and B. K. Sarkar constantly refuted the efforts of Western Indologists and social anthropologists to try to interpret Indian reality in the evolutionary reductionist matrix. Seal thought institutions could only be compared when they were historically coexistent and parallel, and Mukerjee thought Indian social institutions to be unique. He found the sociological categories of West inadequate for the interpretation of the Indian reality. (Singh 2004: 96)

Almost all the early sociologists of India have followed the empirical tradition of sociology. However, some have shown exceptional talent in critiquing the Western sociological paradigm and theoretic structure, while others have shown no special interest in theoretical critique and confined themselves to the empirical studies of micro-social systems. Ghurye, for instance, contributed to sociological writings over several decades and his works cover a vast range of themes relating to the study of rural and urban communities, a tribal community called Mahadev Kolis, Rajput architecture, problems of North-East India, Indian costumes, Bharatanatyam and its costume, Indian sadhus and so on. Ghurye, in brief, expressed through his writings a unique sensitivity to Indian civilisation and explored field-level knowledge on the processes of social change and conflict, cultural styles (dress and fashion) and traditional social formations and sects such as the sadhus and *sampradayas* (see Bibliographical Supplement). However Ghurye remained an empiricist and never showed much interest in abstract theorisation. His empiricist bias is reflected in the syllabus he prepared for the Bombay University post-graduate course where he completely neglected theory and even research methodology (Upadhya 2007: 223). The imprint of Ghurye's sociology can be described as an Indological approach to the study of Indian society combined with empiricism and an emphasis on fieldwork. Ghurye made use of varied methodologies in his empirical studies ranging from empirical surveys to uses of historical materials and traditional Indological texts. Ghurye was a Sanskrit scholar and he turned routinely to classical texts for understanding all manner of contemporary phenomena—costume, architecture, sexuality, urbanism, family and kinship, Indian tribal cultures, the caste system, ritual and religion. Apart from his individual research, Ghurye trained his students to follow his approach to sociology and either encouraged them to study social customs and norms through the study of classical texts (Srinivas 1973: 138) or he sent students to various regions of India to conduct fieldwork on a wide range of topics, usually on a minimal budget. As Srinivas put it, from his chair

Ghurye 'directed a one-man ethnographic survey of India' (*ibid.*). There are similarities between Nirmal Kumar Bose's approach to sociology and social anthropology and Ghurye's empirical approach. Bose, like Ghurye, conducted several empirical studies on concrete structures such as rural and urban communities, culture and communities, Indian temples and their architecture, anthropology of caste and tribes and social change and development. Like Ghurye, Bose was also a diffusionist. Diffusionism is the transmission of elements from one culture to another. Such elements are transmitted by agents using identifiable media and are subject to different barriers or filter effects. As Upadhya writes of the time when Ghurye met Rivers (around 1920):

> Rivers had been converted to the extreme version of diffusionism. Diffusionism had emerged as a critique of late-nineteenth century evolutionism and enjoyed a brief but intense period of popularity in England during the period 1910–30. While evolutionism held that every society would eventually advance towards civilisation, passing through definite stages of cultural development, diffusionists argued that culture was transmitted mainly by the migration of different races, and that "cultural diversity within an area was prima facie evidence that its inhabitants were a racially diverse collection of migrant settlers". (Kuklick 1983: 67 cited in Upadhya 2007: 205)

Ghurye had high regard for Rivers and largely adopted his diffusionist line. In fact, he was so deeply affected by River's sudden death in June 1922 that he described it as the 'biggest tragedy' of his life (Srinivas 1995: 3). Bose was also a diffusionist, but he was more influenced by American anthropologists like A. L. Kroeber and considered Franz Boas as one of his gurus in anthropology (Sinha 1973: 1); Boas established cultural relativism as a governing point within anthropology, and Kroeber was his student.

Both Ghurye and Bose placed more emphasis in the collection of facts than on theorisation. Ghurye's empiricism taught him that the 'facts' would speak for themselves. Bose, even quite late in his life, believed that the primary role of a sociologist was to collect detailed and comprehensive information on a particular theme and expressed his conviction that once this was done, any theoretical proposition could be attempted (Bose 1960: vii). Ghurye's books corroborate his keen interest in empiricism and he crams his writings with a great deal of information without any organisation, analysis or interpretation, leaving the reader in the dark about his argument or rationale. Because of his ill health Ghurye was unable to conduct fieldwork himself, but he employed his students to do fieldwork and directed field-based studies of social change in rural India, the impact of urbanisation as well as ethnographic studies of Mahadev Kolis (Ghurye 1957, 1960, 1963). Bose, after he became the Director of Anthropological Survey of India, initiated several projects to collect information about caste, rural crafts, and social change in modern India.

The third similarity between Ghurye and Bose was that both were nationalist, though their nationalism varied in intensity and character. As Singh (1986: 5–6) has argued, nationalism provided an ideological basis for most of the early sociologists, who attempted in different ways to demonstrate the organic unity of Indian society. Ghurye's sociology provides a prime example of this quest. Ghurye's principal concern in sociology was to demonstrate the unity and antiquity of Indian civilisation. He believed that Hinduism formed the civilisational unity of India and that Brahminical ideas and values which constituted the core of Hinduism were essential for the integration of society (Venugopal 1986). Ghurye's orientalist inclinations, as earlier discussed, influenced him to believe that it was through religion that Indian civilisation was formed as diverse groups were assimilated into Brahminical Hinduism and incorporated into the caste system. Like Bose, Ghurye also believed that Indian culture developed as a product of the acculturation process where the non-Hindu groups were absorbed into Hindu society. Bose called this acculturation process as the Hindu method of tribal absorption. Upadhya views Ghurye's sociology as the progenitor of Hindu nationalist sociology. She writes: 'In short, following the orientalist view and some streams of nationalist discourse,

Ghurye defined Indian society as an essentially Hindu society and its cultural and religious unity as the basis of the nation—a sociological view that underwrote his later political writings' (Upadhya 2007: 215). Ghurye thus played a major role in the institutionalisation of a sociology that reproduced his vision of the nation rooted in Hindu tradition. His sociology was shaped by a complex mix of nationalist, orientalist, reformist ideals systematised through the diffusionist and empiricist framework.

Bose was also a diffusionist, empiricist and nationalist, but his perspective was different. As a nationalist he belonged to the Gandhian school of thought and though like Ghurye he also believed in national unity, his notion of unity was more pluralistic in nature. Bose's solution to the vexed problem of nation-building argues for unity in the economic domain and pluralism in the cultural sphere. However, as the essay in this book argues, Bose's description of caste was reworked and systematised through certain normative ideals of Hinduism which were typically Brahminical in nature. Though Bose expressed his faith and conviction in diffusion and acculturation, his depiction of Hinduism describes a process which vertically integrates different groups into a social structure administered and guided by Brahminical ideals and values. The same vision of the absorptive power of Hinduism explains his argument that tribals were successfully assimilated into the Hindu fold (Bose 1967: 203–215). In a way Bose, like early orientalist writers, projected Indian social history as essentially the history of Hinduism.

The combination of empiricism, orientalism, and reformism produced a type of sociology in India which can be viewed more significantly as a sign of Western power over the Orient rather than as a scientific discourse corresponding with reality. An academic sociology of cultures, ideas, institutions, hence, has to interrogate and examine the hidden power configurations in the studies produced. David Kopf has argued that Nehru was much impressed by the work of orientalists and used their knowledge to build up a nationalistic new India (Kopf 1980: 496). The fact remains that orientalism has been the grist for the mill of nationalism. It is also interesting to note that in contemporary times orientalist ideas of Indianness have been adapted to the self-identities of Indians. Ideas like envisaging the Vedic times as the golden age, spiritual India, caste-centricity and Hinduism as one religion are, at least to some extent, orientalist inventions and more or less largely accepted by Indians as such or reworked to serve Indian nationalism. The influence of orientalist ideas in social thinking consequently has produced 'internal orientalism' which seems to be the most problematic issue in postcolonial scholarship in India. Orientalist ideas and categories still have such power that it is exceedingly difficult for either Indians or outsiders to view India without reverting to the outdated discourse. Orientalist ideas of difference and division have for long infected the foundations of public life in India. It has been rightly observed that in the postcolonial era, 'orientalism without colonialism is a headless theoretical beast, that [is] much harder to identify and eradicate because it has become internalized in the practices of the postcolonial state, the theories of the postcolonial intelligentsia and political action of postcolonial mobs' (Breckenridge and van der Veer 1994: 11).

In comparison, the Lucknow School of sociology was much more theoretically and philosophically oriented. This is evident in the contributions of Radhakamal Mukerjee, Dhurjati Prasad Mukerji and Awadh Kishore Saran. These sociologists displayed much better critical awareness of Western categories and concepts and often rejected them because they thought these categories were inappropriate for India. Radhakamal Mukerjee's vision of sociology, though rooted in the Indian tradition, was still universalistic. He saw the possibility of developing a general theory of sociology based on a social action theory. In the Indian case this theory would be derived from Indian philosophy and tradition. Ghurye was a Sanskrit scholar whereas Mukerjee was educated at Calcutta University. He was, in fact, one among the first group of students to obtain a master's degree in economics and sociology at Calcutta University in 1910 (Madan 2011: 120). In his autobiography Mukerjee recalls that the combined course of economics and sociology was introduced in 1908 at the initiative of the vice-chancellor Asutosh Mukerjee. He writes that he 'found sociology deeper, more comprehensive and more satisfying. I went several times through Comte, Herbert Spencer, Marx, Lester Ward, Giddings and Ross' (Mukerjee 1997: 68). Mukerjee was a voracious reader and during this time he read medieval and modern philosophers as well as classical economists of Europe along with works of the intellectuals of the late nineteenth and early twentieth-century Bengal. Mukerjee writes: 'Somehow an integrated study of the various social sciences of Economics, Political Science, Social Philosophy and Sociology stimulated in me the desire and striving to envisage man, society and civilisation as wholes that defeat any compartmentalization and its aims' (*ibid.*). Dhurjati Prasad likewise had training in history and economics, he obtained post-graduate degrees in both subjects from Calcutta University (he got his history degree in 1918 and economics degrees in 1920) and presumably he too attended the sociology classes that Mukerjee attended. He also believed in the interdisciplinary approach to the study of social sciences and both argued that systems and theories of Indian sociology should be rooted in the specificities of Indian culture. Radhakamal's interpretation of Indian culture was Brahminic and upper-caste, whereas Dhurjati Prasad believed in a 'synthetic' Hindu-Muslim culture (Mukerji 1948). Madan writes:

> The convergences of viewpoint were more than matched by differences. For Radhakamal, the social was embedded in the cosmic; consequently, his robust empiricism was in the ultimate analysis tempered by intuitive understandings. He was a deeply religious person. Contrastively, DP was an agnostic ... He resisted being labelled as a Marxist, conceding no more than being a "Marxologist".... Unlike Radhakamal, he never engaged in fieldwork or survey research, but concentrated on exercises in conceptual clarification and historical interpretations. It is not hard to imagine that the two men, so different temperamentally and in their methodological

> orientation, gradually drifted apart, and DP created his own space. (Madan 2011a: 31)

There is, however, another crucial difference between Radhakamal and Dhurjati Prasad, and that is Radhakamal never had the kind of robust grasp of the politics of his times that Dhurjati Prasad had. Dhurjati Prasad's knowledge of society and history was based on politics and he had better insight and understanding of the production of intellectuals in India, who he thought were a product of the historical encounter with the West. That is why he stressed the need to problematise 'tradition' as an ideological stance implying rootedness in history. For him 'traditionalisms' did not mean adherence to tradition (Hegde 2011).

Radhakamal Mukerjee was not averse to empiricism and conducted important empirical studies on land problems, town and village life, ecology, food planning, institutional planning, population control, migration, etc. He made valuable contributions to both policy-oriented research and meta-theoretic reflections. What is interesting is that his involvement in micro-empirical sociology coexisted with his predilection towards a metaphysical view of man, human society and social institutions. In his typical meta-theoretical style he tended to view man, society and values as an apparent trinity but quintessentially an indivisible unity. Mukerjee acknowledges that he was deeply influenced by two persons, both of whom were scholars of exceptional merit: Brajendranath Seal (1864–1938) and Patrick Geddes (1854–1932). Brajendranath taught philosophy at Calcutta University and Geddes taught sociology and civics at Bombay University. Radhakamal describes Seal as a 'legend in intellectual Bengal', venerated widely for his 'encyclopaedic knowledge'. He admired Seal for having blended the universal with the nationalistic outlook and considered him to be one of the undisputed leaders of the intellectual revolution. Radhakamal was much influenced by Seal's comparative method which, according to him, stressed the multi-linear character of human social evolution in different regions and cultures. For him, Seal's method 'challenged the Hegelian unilinear view of the evolution of mankind and its institutions. It was this synthetic and comparative view which governs my comparative study of economic and political institutions' (Mukerjee 1997: 88). Radhakamal claims that he enriched and extended Seal's comparative methodology in the light of new branches of human discipline such as human ecology, social psychology, cultural anthropology, human geography and biology.

Radhakamal acknowledges Patrick Geddes as one of the greatest minds he encountered, which was marked by a remarkable quickness, vitality and comprehensiveness of thinking (*ibid.*: 95). Mukerjee admits that it was from Geddes he learned the significance of 'social mapping and charting', 'regional planning' and the interplay of 'Place-work-Folk' or 'Environment-Function-Organism', which, for him was 'most revealing '(Mukerjee 1997: 95–96). It is interesting to note here that Ghurye was not much impressed by Geddes. While speaking of Geddes's lectures he wrote in his autobiography: 'I could get nothing more out of them than that place created or dictated work and moulded the people who in their turn conditioned their own work and both in the process modified the place' (Ghurye 1973: 37). It is quite evident that Radhakamal was far more conversant with the Western economic, sociological and philosophical tradition than Ghurye, whose main strength lay in his command over Sanskrit and his scholarship in classical Sanskrit texts. In fact, unlike Radhakamal, Ghurye showed little familiarity with international social science. Referring to the rich body of Western scholarship in the sociology of religion, Pramanick comments: 'Where does Ghurye fit in this theoretical world? Perhaps nowhere' (1994: 144)!

Like Radhakamal, Dhurjati Prasad was well versed in Western social science and critically aware of its limitations. He also believed like Radhakamal in the relevance of Indian tradition and philosophy for arriving at valid theoretical and conceptual schemes for the study of Indian society. He was, however, sceptical about empirical research because he believed empiricism without the knowledge of history and deductive reason can only be superficial. Somewhat jokingly he used to say about himself that 'when sociologists try to spread smoke then I am an economist – because except jurisprudence no other social science other than economics has so much intellectual rigour. And when economists try to spread smoke about mathematics, I want to remind them about social reality' (Mukerji 1956; 1987 (Vol. 3): 136). All his life Dhurjati Prasad thought of himself as a student seeking knowledge and in his own way he tried to harmonise different knowledges, sometimes successfully, sometimes unsuccessfully. But he never wanted to be a specialist. He narrates his position in the following manner: 'During the first World War a song became very popular in Rambagan (in Calcutta): "This is not a cucumber nor a banana darling that I will slice it and give you a share". Division of knowledge is prostitution of intellect and the so-called specialists are like concubines' (*ibid.*: 137). Late in his life, in *Diversities* he wrote:

> My readers think that my interests are more than one sided, ... and that it would have been better if they were limited to one or two. But that is exactly my difficulty. I was trained to think in large terms. It made me look closely into details, but it made me search for the wood behind the trees. My professors, friends and people I have met made me feel that largeness of the canvas. I could not take anything but a synoptic view. Right from the start I had accepted the synthesis of the social sciences, and it has followed me ever since. (Mukerji 2002: viii)

About his own writings, he wrote in his last book *Jhilimili* (1961):

> I have written nineteen books including this one. I could have written one or two more, if health permitted. I don't know what I have written. But it seems there is a broad line. This can be called personality – this is reflected in [my] novels, sociology, economics, history and music. Around this is Karl Marx. In my life influence of Marxism is more. In sociology, history, Marxism is still trendy, that is why I still write. The same can be found in my novels also. I can call myself a Marxologist. In India this is an exceptional thing that is why I am exceptional. (Mukerji 1965; 1987 (Vol. 3): 217–218)

Dhurjati Prasad used the dialectical-historical perspective of 'Marxology' in his writings, especially for the study of the middle class structure and its formation in India. He also analyses the processes of social change and planning in the country and demonstrates the relationship between the Indian tradition and Western conceptual frame of analysis. However as Singh writes: 'But he does not show the same degree of interest, Radhakamal Mukerjee did, about offering a general theoretical paradigm of sociology rooted in the Indian philosophy, history and traditions, as a counterpoint to the western theoretical approaches' (Singh 2004: 145). However, Dhurjati Prasad was trained in history and economics, he had good knowledge of Indian classical music and he was also a literary writer and novelist. His approach to sociological writing was more innovative, imaginative and inventive. This led him to write on sociology of music, modern Indian culture, Indian youth—subjects which were not conventionally popular during his times.

Towards the end of his academic career Mukerji came back to the question of tradition and stressed on the question of self-awareness of Indian sociologists. For Mukerji consciousness of one's tradition takes precedence over any kind of technical knowledge and there can be no substitute for such internal knowledge. As Madan writes: 'Mukerji does not say that the view from within provides complete sociological understanding, only that without it one cannot hope to begin right' (Madan 2013: 152; see also Madan 2011). As discussed in this book Dhurjati Prasad replaces the self-oriented, choice-making individual (*vyakti*) of Western sociology by the other-oriented, group-influenced person (*purusha*) of Indian tradition. The notion of tradition has played a significant role in the ideology of social structure in India. Reorientation of tradition articulated by Dhurjati Prasad reflects the quest for Indian identity in the face of challenges from the paradigms of Western sociology. In his view tradition is not an obstacle to modernisation but a condition which provides us the choice and opportunity to evolve a cultural pattern that can be a synthesis of old and new. Hence modernity has to be defined in relation to, and not in denial of, tradition.

As we have seen, some traditionalists like G. S. Ghurye have been seen as progenitors of Hindu nationalist sociology, but it will be wrong to criticise the Lucknow group of sociologists in the same vein for their unfailing reliance on Brahminical and Sanskrit notions of Indian tradition, as, for example, Oommen (2007) does. While Madan cautions us against speaking casually of the 'Lucknow School' of sociology. 'There really was no "school" formally proclaimed, nor did the faculty share a common approach to teaching and research' (Madan 2007: 261). However the question of how one defines and marks out a school or a tradition can also depend on certain commonalities about wider theoretical and ideological concerns. Certain specific characteristics of this school, through which its practitioners can be identified are: emphasis on civilisational and historical categories in their vision of sociology; theoretical opposition to certain premises of Western sociology, like, positivism, utilitarianism and general evolutionary constructions; introduction of the perspectives of historicity, culture and values in the formulation of sociological concepts and their theoretical underpinnings; open-ended methodological perspective and a broadly inclusive strategy of research.

Both Radhakamal and Dhurjati Prasad made important contributions towards the philosophical critique of the human condition and contemporary civilisation from a holistic perspective. They made use of Indian philosophical concepts, but their approach remained universalistic as both attempted to integrate epistemological concerns of Indian philosophy with those of the West to evolve a general and integral theory of sociology. They attempted a universal theory of society from within the resources of Indian civilisation. The Lucknow School for some constituted an innovative intellectual response to India's colonial subjection and cultural subjugation (Joshi 1986). Hegde mentions three claims of the Lucknow School which constitute its most fundamental convictions: the first was *ontological*, which affirmed that the Indian social order was to be conceived as a field of historicity; the second was *methodological*, which stressed a need to theorise the logics of being discernible in Indian history; and the last was *epistemological*, which asserted the role of tradition in understanding change in Indian society and in doing so, abandoning colonial ideologies and extant Western modes of theorising (Hegde 2011: 53–54).

It is in this context that the essays in this book highlight both Radhakamal's and Dhurjati Prasad's conception of man and their stringent critique of the Western ideology of the individual. Dhurjati Prasad contrasts 'individual' to 'person' following Emmanuel Mousier (1905–1950). An individual is atomistic, egocentric, inauthentic, materialistic, with no sense of value or vocation in life. A person is the opposite, freely adopts the values by which to live and relate to others in a spirit of community. To be a person involves having a set of values freely adopted. It involves creativity and communion with others. Dhurjati Prasad calls this person *purusha* and distinguishes it from the conception of *vyakti* or individual. This is a holistic conception of man. In Radhakamal's writings also we find that the Indian man prefers to merge his individual existence, bereft of all ego-attributes and values, in the transcendent cosmic process. Radhakamal considers his view of man and cosmos as superior to that of the West, because he believes that Indians possess the capacity to view reality in a disinterested and detached manner. He bestows Indian knowledge traditions with a disinterested ontological approach to reality. Both the sociologists showed exceptional modern thinking in their critique of the individual and more importantly made a serious critical and philosophical diagnosis of the crisis of human condition in the industrial societies and its civilisations. Their understanding of the modern individual as objectified, analysed and fixed is contemporary and requires serious analysis. I have tried to show in this book that this objectified conception of the individual has similarities with Foucault's views who believed that the individual is the effect and object of a certain crossing of power and knowledge.

The individual is the product of the complex strategic development in the field of power and multiple developments in the human sciences. That is why Dhurjati Prasad wanted to replace the idea of the regimented individual by a freer, more open, expansive conception of man or *purusha*. He said: 'Our conception of freedom is different because our conception of man is *purusha* and not the individual, or *vyakti*' (Mukerji 2002: 269). Both argue in different ways that to be modern is not to accept oneself as objectified and slotted but to take oneself as the object of a complex and difficult elaboration. Radhakamal in many of his writings compares and contrasts the East and the West, and his epistemological aspirations are rooted in this comparative conceptualisation. His idea of man derived from the reconciliation of opposite tendencies, is free, all-encompassing, and universal. In fact Radhakamal's principal complaint against modern social science was that it was unable to cope with the reconciliation of the great opposites (Mukerjee 1965: 148).

Both sociologists' accounts of the construction of the individual as object and their alternative conceptions of man, *purusha* and person raise important questions about social sciences. More accurately, we can say that their arguments opened up possible avenues for deeper epistemological questions and interrogation. However, the politics of knowledge production in India made these knowledges obscure, inconsequential and minor. Madan, for example, evaluates Radhakamal's work in the following manner: 'As a pioneer, Mukerjee was a man in a great hurry who wrote a great deal on a wide variety of subjects, but did not go deeply into any of them' (Madan 2007: 286). Elsewhere Madan approvingly quotes A. K. Saran who said: 'In his intellectual career Dr. Mukerjee has tried to meet the challenge of West almost in all forms in which it has come', but without noteworthy success because he 'is not a deep thinker' (Saran 1958: 1018, cited in Madan 2011a: 38). In fact Ramkrishna Mukherjee was closer to the truth when he wrote in 1989 that Radhakamal Mukerjee was a *bratya*, that is, an outcast, a marginalised figure, in Indian social sociology. His marginality, according to Ramkrishna Mukherjee, was a consequence of his unconventional views on the nature of social science which was annoying to both economists and sociologists (Mukherjee 1989: 261). By the late eighties when Ramkrishna Mukherjee was writing this, the narrow empiricist sociology had taken such a hold on Indian social science that earlier theorisation on tradition, individual, man and history was considered speculative, tentative and conjectural.

Both Radhakamal and Dhurjati Prasad's critiques of the Western notion of the human condition are at one and the same time historico-theoretical analyses of the limits imposed on us and also an experiment with the possibility of going beyond them. In this they made productive use of Indian concepts and ideas. Our historical ontology is governed by three axes whose specificity and interconnections have to be analysed: the axis of knowledge, the axis of ethics and the axis of power. Both Radhakamal and Dhurjati Prasad have examined in their works the question of knowledge and ethics in great detail, but not so much the question of power. Their critique was directed to the question which can be formulated as how we Indians are constituted as subjects of colonial knowledge. Gradual oblivion of this school of thought put a stop to further enquiries regarding the question of power.

The categories and theories that structured colonial social science (and assiduously followed in Ghurye's sociology) were questioned and confronted by the Lucknow School, which consciously tried to move away from the colonial system of ideas to devise a language of sociology that was simultaneously universal and particular and infused with Indian categories and concepts. The narrow empiricist sociology that succeeded the Lucknow School's ambitious approach made irrelevant large number issues that were considered important in the previous era. It may be that the changed target then was not to discover what we are, but to refuse what we are as Foucault once said (Foucault 2000: 336). Radhakamal in many ways critiqued the ethnocentrism of the Western social theory that placed India in a position of cultural inferiority and dependence. Thakur rightly asserts that Radhakamal was against the extension of the positivistic-utilitarian tradition of the Western social science because of its nominalistic philosophical assumptions. Radhakamal believed that such assumptions accorded a place of pride to the concept of individual that actually did not do justice to Indian values and traditions (Thakur 2014: 163). On the other hand, he wanted to employ Indian principles to create a universal sociological theory. Radhakamal privileged the uniqueness of Indian values in his attempted critique of Western modernity and highlighted the centrifugal, communitarian, non-hedonistic character of Indian culture and polity. In his late writings he wanted Indian sociology to exhibit the larger concerns of social philosophy.

Suddenly, following Independence the Lucknow brand of sociology sank into obscurity and a new phase of Indian sociology began. The decade of 1950s witnessed a proliferation in studies of Indian villages. These studies were empiricist and observational in orientation, descriptive and holistic in nature; villages were considered as microcosms of Indian reality and a detailed descriptive account was supposed to present the sociological reality of India at the ground level. These studies had no theoretical orientation, mainly depended on micro-descriptions and were not analytical in nature. A related change was increased attention towards the tools and techniques of research and the thinking that technology can guide research problems rather than any proper theoretical conceptual framework. The essay on Ramkrishna Mukherjee in this book presents a typical instance of this orientation. Following Independence the object and conception of sociology in India changed drastically and narrow empiricism and methodology became dominant concerns of sociology. Thakur, rather provocatively, asserts that part of the reason for the obscurity of the Lucknow School was that the 'Srinivasian blueprint of Indian sociology would entertain no dissenting/alternative voices lest the architecture of the discipline that M. N. Srinivas and his followers had so assiduously constructed developed internal cracks and eventual collapse' (Thakur 2014: 12). Others have pointed out that the Lucknow sociologists did not receive any sympathetic attention because they were accused of being abstruse, oriented towards ethics and philosophy, they were steeped in parochialism because they actually wanted to develop 'an Indian science of sociology' and as Hegde points out, 'some even going on to insist that the point of departure for any serious sociological enquiry is and ought to remain 'the present and not the past' (Béteille 2002: 206 cited in Hegde 2011: 57), the implication being that the 'traditionalism of the Lucknow School tended to displace Indian sociology to a world that *was* than a world that *is*'.

More generally it is possible to say that following Independence, the epistemic structures and programmes of mainstream social sciences have been closely attached to, and shaped by, the experience of modern-nation state formation in India. It is in this context that the assumption of methodological nationalism becomes important; this is the assumption that considers the nation/state/society as the natural social and political form of the modern world (Wimmer and Schiller 2002). The insidious effects of methodological nationalism were visible, for example, in fields like anthropology and sociology in India as the discipline turned towards functionalism from the 1950s. Anthropologists and sociologists assumed that the cultures to be studied were unitary and organically related to, and fixed within territories, thus reproducing the image of the social world divided into bounded, culturally specific units typical of nationalist thinking. The empiricist fact-finding project of village studies fulfilled such ambitions.

While the efforts of the Lucknow sociologists demonstrated that it was perfectly possible to explore, and aspire for, a universal language of social science from within the tradition, to work out a synthetic integrated model which could both retain the 'Eastern' tradition and yet surpass the West's modernity, the naturalisation of the nation-state in different disciplines compartmentalised the social science project. Under the circumstances sociology became obsessed with describing the process within nation-state boundaries and lost sight of its international dimension. For Srinivas, for example, sociology meant the study of Indian society, and everything extending its borders was cut off analytically. The container society encompasses a culture, a polity, and a bounded social group. This particular perspective produced adverse consequences because of the methodological limitation of the analytical horizon, thus removing trans-border connections and processes from the picture.

Artificial boundaries of sociology produced spurious technical solutions to sociological research in India. The practice of empiricism in its extreme form lead to attempts which promoted positivistic, technological solutions as the be-all and end-all for sociological enquiry. Ramkrishna Mukherjee is a typical representative of the technique-dependent sociologist, though the technique he suggests is full of theoretical errors as the chapter on Mukherjee shows. Ironically in his early academic life Mukherjee followed a dialectical-Marxian approach to social science and wrote a book on *The Rise and Fall of the East Indian Company* (1958), which was a contribution to economic and social history of the institutionalisation of colonialism in India through stabilisation of economic policies, disintegration of feudalism and aristocratic despotism, and the rise of new middle classes. Published one year earlier, in his *The Dynamics of Rural Society* (1957) Mukherjee studied social and economic changes in a set of villages through changes in the structure of classes. In his other studies of rural society, Mukherjee made use of empirical data to formulate and analyse the class structure to unravel the problem of rural India from a quasi-Marxist perspective (Mukherjee 1957, 1971; see Bibliographical Supplement for his other works). In his later works Mukherjee changed from a dialectical-Marxian orientation to a positivistic-inductivist approach which, according to him, was based on five questions: What is it? How is it? Why is it? What will it be? What should it be? These questions respectively explain and elaborate the following: enumeration of the phenomenon, classification, causality, possibility and desirability. It is interesting to note that Mukherjee evaluates the growth of Indian sociology in terms of these five questions and points out that the modernisers, that is the sociologists from the 1950s who came after the 'pioneers', 'hardly ever looked beyond the societal characteristics which were clearly observable, and thus failed to consider systematically the "what", "how", "why", "what will it be", and "what should it be" questions within the total framework of society' (Mukherjee 1979a: 52). In contrast the pioneers (including the Lucknow sociologists) followed theoretical formulations which, according to him, were not unsystematic and 'abstract generalisations about Man and Society' (*ibid.*: 39).

Mukherjee carried out an effacement of the older genre of theory by shifting the focus from 'theory of research' to 'technology of research'. His inductive-inferential method is a tool of research, a technology, it is an attempt to demonstrate that the discipline of sociology is 'scientific' and thus he tries to legitimise the 'scientific' status of sociology. But this aspiration has failed in the past because of the notion of positivism that it carries. On the other hand sociologists influenced by ordinary language philosophy undermine the empiricist conception of language upon which quantitative description is said to rely.

The men who headed the new sociology departments that were created during the rapid expansion of universities following Independence realised that their academic acceptance depended in demonstrating that their discipline was 'scientific' and useful for the state. The reasons for emphasis in methodology emerged from such specificities of the new phase of sociology in India. Singh has rightly pointed out that the new phase of sociology that was ushered after Independence was characterised by the 'unprecedented growth in methodological consciousness in the discipline and the teaching of methodology began as a specialized course at most places' (Singh 2004: 146). Through his inductive-inferential method, Mukherjee devised a tool or a technology of research which was independent of type of proposition; its purpose was to test and verify propositions independent of their ideology (Mukherjee 1975). However, comparing two different kinds of theoretical propositions demands a language into which at least the empirical consequences of both can be translated without loss or change. It is possible to argue that proponents of different theories speak different languages, languages expressing different cognitive commitments, suitable for different worlds. Mukherjee's technology itself is not a transparent tool and it is ideologically loaded. Theories, on the other hand, expressed in different 'languages', that is incommensurable theories cannot be compared on their empirical implications.

The book describes three different trajectories of twentieth-century Indian sociology and delineates three different orientations. The first was the sociology of G. S. Ghurye, shared to some extent by N. K. Bose, which was a complex mix of nationalist, reformist, orientalist ideals organised through the diffusionist and empiricist framework. This sociology was the progenitor of Hindu nationalist sociology, whose political ramifications are still strong and visible in contemporary India. The second stream was the sociology of the Lucknow School, where the purpose was to legislate a distinct role of sociological enquiry in India that could occupy a distinct space between nationalism and internationalism. In their efforts towards such a mediation Lucknow sociologists added a new perspective towards the politics of decolonisation for the newly emerging independent nations of the mid-twentieth century. Their vision of sociology, though rooted in the Indian tradition, was still universalistic in orientation. They visualised the possibility of developing a general theory of sociology derived from Indian philosophy and tradition. Anticipating the idea of 'provincializing Europe' the Lucknow sociologists seriously explored the capacities and limitations of the Western social and political categories in the context of Indian life-worlds. Hegde rightly points out that the question of modernity and modernisation is not just a 'sociological problem of historical transition' but a 'problem of translation as well' (Chakrabarty 2001: 17). Hegde writes:

> The founders of the Lucknow School seem to grasp this, so that in urging the Indian sociologist to be an Indian first they were concerned to mediate a position for sociology that would take tradition and traditionalism seriously and in the process "translate" apparently incoherent forms of modernity into their own categories. (Hegde 2011: 65)

This was the most promising line of sociological enquiry of the Lucknow School. However, from the mid-twentieth century it fell into obscurity under the influence of narrow empiricism and excessive stress on 'realistic', field-based study of micro social institutions. Under the strong influence of such a 'regime of truth' the Lucknow sociologists were considered speculative, conjectural, and blamed wrongly for their reliance on Brahminical and Sanskritic notions of Indian tradition (Oommen 2007). This narrow empiricist sociology lead into a blind alley that is represented by Ramkrishna Mukherjee's pronouncements on inductive-inferential methodology.

Surely it is not possible to replicate the model of the Lucknow School in today's India; however, the Lucknow School's ethic of indignity deserves our serious attention. The quest towards indignity is always a move towards reciprocity in knowledge production. Reciprocity in social thinking neutralises asymmetric relationships in knowledge formation. The concepts and the process of conceptualisation by the Lucknow School create new options for thought and new possibilities for action. Take, for example, their conceptualisation of man wherein they attempt to unify diverse domains under a common term. Most importantly they critiqued the dominant knowledges of their times, knowledges which were governed by certain rules that established what could be said truthfully, the criteria of evidence, the forms of proof and even the very object of which one could speak. Their writings alert us to the crucial question: what should be the sociology of the present? How can sociology create, produce and intensify possibilities within existence? I hope this book has in its own way prepared us for this task.

REFERENCES

Barthes, Roland. 1977. *Image-Music-Text,* trans. Stephen Heath. London: Fontana.

Béteille, André. 1975. 'Introduction'. In *The Structure of Hindu Society,* Nirmal Kumar Bose, trans. André Béteille. 1–21. New Delhi: Orient Longman.

———. 1997. 'Newness in Sociological Enquiry'. *Sociological Bulletin* 46(1): 97–110.

———. 2002. *Sociology: Essays on Approach and Method.* New Delhi: Oxford University Press.

Black, Max. 1954. '"Pragmatic" Justification of Induction'. In *Problems of Analysis: Philosophical Essays,* ed. Max Black. 157–190. London: Routledge and Kegan Paul.

———. 1958. 'Self-supporting Inductive Arguments'. *The Journal of Philosophy* 55: 718–725.

Bose, Nirmal Kumar. 1927. 'Spring Festival of India'. *Man in India* 7(2–3): 112–155.

———. 1932. *Canons of Orissan Architecture.* Calcutta: R. Chatterjee.

———. 1934. *Selections from Gandhi.* Ahmedabad: Navajivan Trust.

———. 1935. 'Bharate Nritatva Charachar Ekti Adhyay'. In *Rajatjayanti: Bharat Samrajer Pachis Batsar,* eds. Kedarnath Chattopadhyay and Sajanikanta Das. 63–65. Calcutta: Bengal Journals.

———. 1940a. 'Prehistoric Research in Mayurbhanj'. *Science and Culture* 6: 75–79.

———. 1940b. *Studies in Gandhism.* Calcutta: D. M. Library.

Bose, Nirmal Kumar. 1949 [1930]. *Nabin o Prachin* (The New and the Old). Calcutta: Bengal Publishers.

______. 1953 [1929]. *Cultural Anthropology and Other Essays*. Calcutta: Indian Associated Publishing Co.

______. 1959. *Modern Bengal*. Calcutta: Vidyodaya Library.

______. 1960a [1926]. *Konaraker Bibaran* (Description of Konarak). Calcutta: Purogami Prakashani.

______. 1960b. *Data on Caste in Orissa*. Calcutta: Anthropological Survey of India.

______. 1961. *Peasant Life in India: A Study in Indian Unity and Diversity*. Delhi: GOI, Manager of Publications.

______. 1965. 'Calcutta: A Pre-mature Metropolis'. *Scientific American* 213(3): 91–102.

______. 1967. *Culture and Society in India*. Bombay: Asia Publishing House.

______. 1968. *Calcutta 1964: A Social Survey*. Bombay: Lalvani Publishing House.

______. 1969. *Problems of Indian Nationalism*. Bombay: Allied Publishers.

______. 1971. *Biallisher Bangla* (Bengal of 1942). Calcutta: Saraswat Library.

______. 1972. *Anthropology and Some Indian Problems*. Calcutta: Institute of Social Research and Applied Anthropology.

______. 1974. *My Days with Gandhi*. Bombay: Orient Longman.

______. 1975 [1949]. *The Structure of Hindu Society* (*Hindu Samajer Garan*), trans. André Béteille. New Delhi: Orient Longman.

______. 1982 [1940]. *Paribrajaker Diary* (A Wanderer's Diary). Calcutta: Dhrupadi.

Bose, Pradip Kumar. 1986. 'Social Research as Inductive Process'. *Economic and Political Weekly* 21(25–26): 1105–1106.

______. 1995. *Research Methodology*. New Delhi: Indian Council of Social Science Research.

______. 1998. *Samayiki: Purono Samayik Patrer Prabandha Sankalan: Bigyan o Samaj* (Selections from Old Bengali Periodicals: Science and Society). Calcutta: Ananda.

Breckenridge, Carol A., and Peter van der Veer. 1994. 'Orientalism and Postcolonial Predicament'. In *Orientalism and Postcolonial Predicament*, eds. Carol A. Breckenridge and Peter van der Veer. 1–22. New Delhi: Oxford University Press.

Carnap, R. 1950. *Logical Foundation of Probability*. Chicago: University of Chicago Press.

______. 1954. 'The Two Concepts of Probability'. *Philosophy and Phenomenological Research* 5(4): 513–532.

Chakrabarty, Dipesh. 2001. *Provincializing Europe: Postcolonial Thought and Historical Difference.* Princeton and Oxford: Princeton University Press.

Chatterjee, Partha. 1995. *The Nation and its Fragments: Colonial and Postcolonial Histories.* Delhi: Oxford University Press.

Clifford, James. 1986a. 'Introduction: Partial Truths'. In *Writing Culture: The Poetics and Politics of Ethnography,* eds. James Clifford and George E. Marcus. 1–26. Berkeley: University of California Press.

______. 1986b. 'On Ethnographic Allegory'. In *Writing Culture: The Poetics and Politics of Ethnography,* eds. James Clifford and George E. Marcus. 98–121. Berkeley: University of California Press.

Cohn, Bernard S. 1971. *India: The Social Anthropology of a Civilization.* Englewood Cliffs, New Jersey: Prentice-Hall.

______. 1990a. 'Notes on the History of the Study of Indian Society and Culture'. In *An Anthropologist among Historians and Other Essays,* Bernard S. Cohn. 136–171. New Delhi: Oxford University Press.

______. 1990b. 'The Census, Social Structure and Objectification in South Asia'. In *An Anthropologist among Historians and Other Essays,* Bernard S. Cohn. 224–254. Delhi: Oxford University Press.

Dow, Alexander. 1970. 'A Dissertation Concerning the Customs, Manners, Language, Religion and Philosophy of the Hindoos'. In *The British Discovery of Hinduism in Eighteenth Century,* ed. P. J. Marshall. 107–139. Cambridge: Cambridge University Press.

Dumont, Louis. 1970 [1966]. *Homo Hierarchicus: The Caste System and its Implications,* trans. Mark Sainsbury. Delhi: Vikas.

______. 1986. *Essays on Individualism: Modern Ideology in Anthropological Perspective.* Chicago: University of Chicago Press.

Feigl, H. 1952. 'Validation and Vindication'. In *Readings in Ethical Theory,* eds. W. Sellers and J. Hospers. 667–680. New York: Appleton Century Crofts.

______. 1963. 'On Meaning and the Limits of Justification'. In *Philosophical Analysis: A Collection of Essays,* ed. Max Black. 113–131. Englewood Cliffs, N. J.: Prentice Hall.

Foucault, Michel. 1972. *Power/Knowledge: Selected Interviews and Other Writings 1972–1977.* New York: Pantheon Books.

______. 1982. 'The Subject and Power'. In *Michel Foucault: Beyond Structuralism and Hermeneutics,* Hubert L. Dreyfus and Paul Rabinow. 208–226. Chicago: The University of Chicago Press.

Foucault, Michel. 1997. *Essential Works of Foucault, Vol. I: Ethics, Subjectivity and Truth*. New York: The New Press.

______. 2000. *Essential Works of Foucault, Vol. III: Power*. London: Allen Lane.

Ghurye, G. S. 1957. *The Mahadev Kolis*. Bombay: Popular Prakashan.

______. 1960. *After a Century and a Quarter: Lonikand Then and Now*. Bombay: Popular Prakashan.

______. 1963. *Anatomy of a Rururban Community*. Bombay: Popular Prakashan.

______. 1969 [1932]. *Caste and Race in India*. Bombay: Popular Prakashan.

______. 1973. *I and Other Explorations*. Bombay: Popular Prakashan.

Hegde, Sasheej. 2011. 'Searching for Bedrock: Contending with the Lucknow School and its Legacy'. In *Doing Sociology in India: Genealogies, Locations and Practices*, ed. Sujata Patel. 47–71. New Delhi: Oxford University Press.

Hegel, G. W. F. 2010. *Philosophy of Right*, trans. T. M. Knox. New York: Digireads.com Publishing.

Hempel, C. G. 1945. 'Studies in the Logic of Confirmation'. *Mind* 54(21): 102–112.

______. 1965. *Aspects of Scientific Explanation*. New York: The Free Press.

______. 1966. 'Recent Problems of Induction'. In *Mind and Cosmos: Essays in Contemporary Science and Philosophy*, ed. Robert G. Colodny. 112–134. Pittsburgh: University of Pittsburgh Press.

Jayaram, N. 2014. 'Against Fragmentation: Radhakamal Mukerjee's Philosophy of Social Science'. *Sociological Bulletin* 63(1): 4–20.

Joshi, P. C. 1986. 'Lucknow School of Economics and Sociology and its Relevance Today: Some Reflections'. *Sociological Bulletin* 35(1): 1–28.

Karve, Irawati. 1968. *Hindu Society: An Interpretation*. Poona: Deshmukh Prakashan.

Keynes, J. M. 1921. *A Treatise on Probability*. London: Macmillan and Co.

Klass, Morton. 1980. *Caste: The Emergence of the South Asian Social System*. Philadelphia: Institute for the Study of Human Issues.

Kopf, David. 1980. 'Hermeneutic versus History'. *Journal of Asian Studies* 3: 496–506.

Kroeber, A. 1971. 'The Super-organic'. *American Anthropologist* 19: 163–213.

Kuklick, Henrika. 1983. 'Tribal Exemplars: Images of Political Authority in British Anthropology, 1885–1945'. In *Observers*

Observed: Essays on Ethnographic Fieldwork, ed. G. Stocking. 59–82. Madison: University of Wisconsin Press.

Kyburg, H. E. 1974. 'Propensity and Probabilities'. *British Journal of Philosophy of Science* 24: 358–375.

Leblanc, Hugues. 1963. 'That Positive Instances are No Help'. *The Journal of Philosophy* 60(16): 453–462.

Lévinas, Emmanuel. 1987. *Emmanuel Lévinas: Collected Philosophical Papers*. The Hague: Martnus Nijhoff.

Ludden, David. 1994. 'Orientalist Empiricism: Transformations of Colonial Knowledge'. In *Orientalism and Postcolonial Predicament*, eds. Carol A. Breckenridge and Peter van der Veer. 250–278. New Delhi: Oxford University Press.

Mackie, J. L. 1963. 'The Paradox of Confirmation'. *The British Journal of Philosophy of Science* 13: 265–277.

Madan, T. N. 2007. 'Search for Synthesis: The Sociology of D. P. Mukerji'. In *Anthropology in the East: Founders of Indian Sociology and Anthropology*, eds. Patricia Uberoi, Nandini Sundar and Satish Deshpande. 256–289. Ranikhet: Permanent Black.

———. 2011. *Sociological Traditions: Methods and Perspectives in the Sociology of India*. New Delhi: SAGE.

———. 2011a. 'Radhakamal Mukerjee and his Contemporaries: Founding Fathers of Sociology in India'. *Sociological Bulletin* 60(1): 18–44.

———. 2013. *Sociology at the University of Lucknow: The First Half Century (1921–1975)*. New Delhi: Oxford University Press.

Mandelbaum, David. 1976. 'Foreword'. In *Aspects of Changing India: Studies in Honour of Prof. G. S. Ghurye*, ed. S. Devadas Pillai. v–viii. Bombay: Popular Prakashan.

Mukerjee, Radhakamal. 1997. *India: The Dawn of a New Era*. New Delhi: Radha Publications.

———. 2005a [1949]. *The Social Structure of Values*. New Delhi: Radha Publications.

———. 2005b [1960]. *The Philosophy of Social Science*. New Delhi: Radha Publications.

———. 2005c [1964]. *The Dimension of Values*. New Delhi: Radha Publications.

———. 2005d [1965]. *The Oneness of Mankind*. New Delhi: Radha Publications.

———. 2006. *The Community of Communities*. New Delhi: Radha Publications.

Mukerji, Dhurjati Prasad. 1931. *Amra o Tahara* (Us and Them). Calcutta: Gupta Friends and Co.

______. 1933. *Chintayasi* (Reflect). Calcutta: Kundabhushan Bhaduri.

______. 1948 [1942]. *Modern Indian Culture.* Bombay: Hind Kitabs.

______. 1954. 'Social Research'. In *Ghurye Felicitation Volume,* ed. K. M. Kapadia. 234–237. Bombay: Popular Prakashan.

______. 1956. *Mone Elo* (Remembrances). Calcutta: New Age.

______. 1957. *Byaktabya* (Utterance). Calcutta: Bidyodaya Library.

______. 1965 [1961]. *Jhilimili* (Twinkling). Calcutta: Indian Associated Publishing.

______. 1987. *Dhurjatiprasad Rachanabali* (Collected Works of Dhurjati Prasad), 3 vols. Calcutta: Dey's Publications.

______. 2002 [1958]. *Diversities: Essays in Economics, Sociology and other Social Problems.* New Delhi: Manak Publications.

______. 2004a [1924]. *Personality and the Social Sciences.* Calcutta: Rupa and Co.

______. 2004b [1932]. *Basic Concepts in Sociology.* Calcutta: Rupa and Co.

Mukherjee, Ramkrishna. 1958. *The Rise and Fall of the East India Company.* Bombay: Popular Prakashan.

______. 1972. 'On the Mode of Social Research'. *The Indian Journal of Sociology* 3(1–2): 55–68.

______. 1975. *Social Indicators.* Delhi: Macmillan and Co.

______. 1979. *What Will It Be? Explorations in Inductive Sociology.* Bombay: Allied Publishers.

______. 1979a. *Sociology of Indian Sociology.* Bombay: Allied Publishers.

______. 1983. *Classifications in Social Research.* Albany: State University of New York.

______. 1989. *The Quality of Life: Valuation in Social Research.* New Delhi: SAGE.

______. 1989a. 'Indian Sociology or Sociology of India?' In *National Tradition in Sociology,* ed. Nikolai Genov. 135–150. New Delhi: SAGE.

______. 1993. *Systematic Sociology.* New Delhi: SAGE.

Mukhopadhyay, Bhudev. 1981 [1892]. *Samajik Prabandha.* Kolkata: Paschimbanga Rajya Pustak Parishad.

Munshi, Srobona, ed. 2009. *Redefining Humanism: Selected Essays of D. P. Mukerji.* New Delhi: Tulika Books.

Narain, Dhirendra. 1979. 'G. S. Ghurye'. *International Encyclopaedia of the Social Sciences (Biographical Supplement)* 18: 238–239.

Oommen, T. K. 2007. *Knowledge and Society: Situating Sociology and Social Anthropology.* New Delhi: Oxford University Press.

Pap, Arthur. 1962. *An Introduction to Philosophy of Science.* New York: The Free Press.

Pillai, S. Devadas. 1976. 'The Sociology of Ghurye'. In *Aspects of Changing India: Studies in Honour of Prof. G. S. Ghurye,* ed. S. Devadas Pillai. 27–40. Bombay: Popular Prakashan.

Pocock, David E. 1960. 'Sociologies: Urban and Rural'. *Contributions to Indian Sociology* 4: 63–81.

Pramanick, S. K. 1982. 'Historical Evolutionary Approach in the Sociology of G. S. Ghurye'. *Sociological Bulletin* 31(1): 24–40.

———. 1994. *Sociology of G. S. Ghurye.* Jaipur: Rawat Publications.

Pratt, Mary Louise. 1986. 'Fieldwork in Common Places'. In *Writing Culture: The Poetics and Politics of Ethnography,* eds. James Clifford and George E. Marcus. 27–50. Berkeley: University of California Press.

Reichenbach, Hans. 1949. *Theory of Probability.* California: University of California Press.

Salmon, W. C. 1961. 'Vindication and Induction'. In *Current Issues in Philosophy of Science,* eds. H. Feigl and G. E. Maxwell. 245–256. New York: Holt, Rinehart and Winston.

———. 1968. 'Inquiries into the Foundations of Science'. In *Vistas in Science,* ed. David L. Arm. 139–158. New Mexico: University of New Mexico Press.

Saran, A. K. 1958. 'India'. In *Contemporary Sociology,* ed. J. S. Roucek. 1013–1034. New York: Philosophical Library.

———. 1997. 'On Modernity'. In *Social and Cultural Diversities: D. P. Mukerji in Memorium,* ed. Abha Avasthi. 55–77. Jaipur: Rawat Publications.

Senart, Émile. 1930 [1896]. *Caste in India: The Facts and the System.* London: Methuen.

Singh, Yogendra. 1983. *Image of Man: Ideology and Theory in Indian Sociology.* Delhi: Chanakya Publications.

———. 1986. 'Indian Sociology'. *Current Sociology* 34(2): 1–50.

———. 2004. *Ideology and Theory in Indian Sociology.* Jaipur: Rawat.

Sinha, Purnima. 2001. *Nirmal Kumar Bose.* Calcutta: Paschimbanga Bangla Academy.

Sinha, Surajit. 1973. *Anthropology of Nirmal Kumar Bose.* Varanasi: Bose Memorial Foundation.

———. 1986. *Nirmal Kumar Bose: Scholar Wanderer.* New Delhi: National Book Trust.

Srinivas, M. N. 1973. 'Itineraries of an Indian Social Anthropologist'. *International Social Science Journal* 25(1–2): 129–148.

Srinivas, M. N. 1995. 'Professor G. S. Ghurye and I: A Troubled Relationship'. In *The Legacy of G. S. Ghurye: A Centennial Festschrift*, ed. A. R. Momin. 1–12. Bombay: Popular Prakashan.

Srinivas, M. N., and M. N. Panini. 1973. 'The Development of Sociology and Social Anthropology in India'. *Sociological Bulletin* 22(2): 179–215.

Strawson, P. F. 1952. *Introduction to Logical Theory*. London: Methuen.

Wesley, W. C. 1963. 'On Vindicating Induction'. In *Induction: Some Current Issues*, eds. H. E. Kyburg and E. Nagel. 211–234. Middletown, Connecticut: Wesleyan University Press.

Tagore, Rabindranath. 1917. *Personality*. New York: Macmillan and Co.

Thakur, Manish. 2014. *The Quest for Indian Sociology: Radhakamal Mukerjee and Our Times*. Shimla: Indian Institute of Advanced Study.

Upadhya, Carol. 2007. 'The Idea of Indian Society: G. S. Ghurye and the Making of Indian Sociology'. In *Anthropology in the East: Founders of Indian Sociology and Anthropology*, eds. Patricia Uberoi, Nandini Sundar and Satish Deshpande. 194–255. Ranikhet: Permanent Black.

Venugopal, C. N. 1986. 'G. S. Ghurye's Ideology of Normative Hinduism'. *Contribution to Indian Sociology* 20(2): 305–314.

______. 1998. *Religion and Indian Society: A Sociological Perspective*. New Delhi: Gyan Publishing House.

Weber, Max. 1958. *The Protestant Ethic and the Spirit of Capitalism*, trans. Talcott Parsons. New York: Scribner's.

Wimmer, Andreas, and Nina Glick Schiller. 2002. 'Methodological Nationalism and Beyond: Nation-state Building, Migration and the Social Sciences'. *Global Networks* 2(4): 301–334.

BIBLIOGRAPHICAL SUPPLEMENT

Radhakamal Mukerjee (1889–1968)

Books in English

The Foundations of Indian Economics. London: Longmans, Green, and Co., 1916.

Principles of Comparative Economics, 2 Vols. London: P. S. King and Sons, 1921.

Democracies of the East: A Study in Comparative Politics. London: P. S. King and Sons, 1923.

Groundwork of Economics. London: Longmans, Green, and Co., 1925.

Borderlands of Economics. London: George Allen and Unwin, 1925.

Civics: Preliminaries of Citizenship: Civic Institutions and Machinery: Civic Parties and Problems. London: Longmans, Green, and Co., 1926.

The Rural Economy of India. London: Longmans, Green, and Co., 1926.

Regional Sociology. New York: The Century Co., 1926.

(With N. N. Sengupta) *Introduction to Social Psychology: Mind in Society*. Boston and New York: Heath and Company, 1928.

Land Problems in India. London: Longmans, Green, and Co., 1933.

Migrant Asia. Rome: Tipografia Failli, 1936.

Theory and Art of Mysticism. London: Longmans, Green, and Co., 1937.

Food Planning for Four Hundred Million. London: Macmillan and Co., 1938.
The Changing Face of Bengal. Calcutta: University of Calcutta, 1938.
The Regional Balance of Man: An Ecological Theory of Population. Madras: University of Madras, 1938.
Man and His Habitation: A Study in Social Ecology. London: Longmans, Green, and Co., 1940.
The Institutional Theory of Economics. London: Macmillan and Co., 1942.
The Food Supply. London: Oxford University Press, 1942.
The Political Economy of Population. London: Longmans, Green, and Co., 1944.
An Economist Looks at Pakistan. Bombay: Hind Kitabs, 1944.
Population Problem in South-East Asia. Allahabad: Kitabistan, 1944.
Social Ecology. London: Longmans, Green, and Co., 1945.
The Economic History of India, 1600–1800. London: Longmans, Green, and Co., 1945.
The Indian Working Class. Bombay: Hind Kitabs, 1945.
Planning the Countryside: First Report. Bombay: Hind Kitabs, 1946.
Races, Land and Food: A Program for World Subsistence. New York: Dryden Press, 1946.
The Social Function of Art. Bombay: Hind Kitabs, 1948.
The Social Structure of Values. London: Macmillan and Co., 1949.
The Dynamics of Morals: A Socio-Psychological Theory of Ethics. London: Macmillan and Co., 1950.
The Horizon of Marriage. Bombay: Asia Publishing House, 1951.
The Indian Scheme of Life. Bombay: Hind Kitabs, 1951.
The Lord of the Autumn Moons. Bombay: Asia Publishing House, 1957.
The Culture and Art of India. London: George Allen and Unwin, 1959.
The Symbolic Life of Man. Bombay: Hind Kitabs, 1959.
The Philosophy of Social Science. London: Macmillan and Co., 1960.
The Dimension of Human Evolution: A Bio-Philosophical Interpretation. London: Macmillan and Co., 1963.
The Philosophy of Personality. Bombay: Allied Publishers, 1963.
The Dimensions of Value: A Unified Theory. London: George Allen and Unwin, 1964.
The Destiny of Civilisation. Bombay: Asia Publishing House, 1964.
The Sickness of Civilisation. Bombay: Allied Publishers, 1964.
The Flowering of Indian Art: The Growth and Spread of a Civilization. Bombay: Asia Publishing House, 1964.
The Oneness of Mankind. London: Macmillan and Co., 1965.

The Cosmic Art of India. Bombay: Allied Publishers, 1965.
A District Town in Transition. Bombay: Asia Publishing House, 1965.
The Community of Communities. Bombay: Manaktalas, 1966.
The Way of Humanism: East and West. Bombay: Academic Press, 1968.
The Song of Self Supreme (Astavakragita). Delhi: Motilal Banarsidass, 1971.
Fundamental Unity of India. Bombay: Bharatiya Vidya Prakashan, 1977.
Society and Community in India. Ajmer: Sachin Publications, 1979.
Bhagavad Gita: The Dialogue with the Self Divine. New Delhi: D. K. Publishers, 1997.
India: The Dawn of a New Era: An Autobiography. New Delhi: Radha Publications, 1997.

Edited Books

Field and Farmers of Oudh. London: Longmans, Green, and Co., 1929.
Economic Problems of Modern India, 2 Vols. London: Macmillan and Co., 1939.
Labour and Planning. Bombay: Asia Publishing House, 1964.
Social Sciences and Planning in India. Bombay: Asia Publishing House.

Govind Sadashiv Ghurye (1893–1983)

Books in English

Caste and Race in India. London: Routledge and Kegan Paul, 1932.
The second and third editions of this book were published with the title *Caste and Class in India* in 1950 and 1956 respectively; the fourth edition was published as *Caste, Class and Occupation* in 1961; and the fifth edition was published as *Caste and Race in India* in 1969. The last four editions were published by Popular Prakashan, Bombay.
The Aborigines, So-called and their Future. Bombay: Popular Prakashan, 1943.
Culture and Society. Bombay: Oxford University Press, 1947.
Occidental Civilization. Bombay: International Book House, 1948.
Indian Costume. Bombay: Popular Prakashan, 1951.
Race Relations in Negro Africa. Bombay: Asia Publishing House, 1952.
Indian Sadhus. Bombay: Popular Prakashan, 1953.

Family and Kin in Indo-European Culture. Bombay: Popular Prakashan, 1955.

Sexual Behaviour of the American Female. Bombay: Popular Prakashan, 1956.

The Mahadev Kolis. Bombay: Popular Prakashan, 1957.

Bharata Natya and its Costume. Bombay: Popular Prakashan, 1958.

The Scheduled Tribes. Bombay: Popular Book Depot, 1959 (first published as *The Aborigines, So-called and their Future,* 1943).

After a Century and a Quarter: Lonikand Then and Now. Bombay: Popular Prakashan, 1960.

Cities and Civilization. Bombay: Popular Prakashan, 1962.

Gods and Men. Bombay: Popular Prakashan, 1962.

Anatomy of a Rururban Community. Bombay: Popular Prakashan, 1963.

Anthropo-Sociological Papers. Bombay: Popular Prakashan, 1963.

The Scheduled Tribes. Bombay: Popular Prakashan, 1963.

Religious Consciousness. Bombay: Popular Prakashan, 1965.

Shakespeare on Conscience and Justice. Bombay: Popular Prakashan, 1965.

Rajput Architecture. Bombay: Popular Prakashan, 1968.

Social Tensions in India. Bombay: Popular Prakashan, 1968.

Two Brahminical Institutions: Gotra and Charana. Bombay: Popular Prakashan, 1972.

I and Other Explorations. Bombay: Popular Prakashan, 1973.

Whither India? Bombay: Popular Prakashan, 1974.

Indian Acculturation: Agastya and Skanda. Bombay: Popular Prakashan, 1977.

India Recreates Democracy. Bombay: Popular Prakashan, 1978.

Legacy of Ramayana. Bombay: Popular Prakashan, 1979.

Vedic India. Bombay: Popular Prakashan, 1979.

Edited Books

(With A. P. Pillay) *Indian Population Problems.* Bombay: Indian Population Conference, 1938.

Books in Marathi

Samaj-Shastra (Social Studies). Poona: Arya Samskriti Mudranalaya, 1949.

Dhurjati Prasad Mukerji (1894–1961)

Books in English

Personality and the Social Sciences. Calcutta: Modern Art Press Publishers, 1924.

Basic Concepts in Sociology. London: Kegan Paul, Trench, Trubner and Co., 1932.

Modern Indian Culture: A Sociological Study, 2nd revised edition. Bombay: Hind Kitabs, 1948. (First edition published from Allahabad in 1942.)

Tagore: A Study. Bombay: Padma Publishers, 1943.

On Indian History: A Study in Method. Bombay: Hind Kitabs, 1945.

Indian Music: An Introduction. Poona: Kutub Publishers, 1945.

Problems of Indian Youth. Bombay: Hind Kitabs, 1946.

Diversities: Essays in Economics, Sociology and Other Social Problems. New Delhi: People's Publishing House, 1958.

Books in Bengali

Amra o Tahara (Us and Them). Calcutta: Gupta Friends and Co., 1931.

Realist. Calcutta: Kundabhushan Bhaduri, 1933.

Chintayasi (Reflect). Calcutta: Kundabhushan Bhaduri, 1933.

Antashila (Subterranean). Calcutta: Kundabhushan Bhaduri, 1935.

Sur o Sangati (Music and Harmony). Calcutta: Kundabhushan Bhaduri, 1935.

Abarta (Eddies). Calcutta: Kundabhushan Bhaduri, 1937.

Katha o Sur (Words and Music). Calcutta: Visvabharati Granthalay, 1938.

Mohana (Estuary). Calcutta: Bharati Bhavan, 1943.

Mone Elo (Remembrances). Calcutta: New Age, 1956.

Byaktabya (Utterance). Calcutta: Bidyodaya Library, 1957.

Jhilimili (Twinkling). Calcutta: Indian Associated Publishing Co., 1961.

Other Collections

Dhurjatiprasad Rachanabali (Collected Works of Dhurjati Prasad), 3 Vols. Calcutta: Dey's Publishing, 1987.

Munshi, Srobona, ed. 2009. *Redefining Humanism: Selected Essays of D. P. Mukerji.* New Delhi: Tulika Books.

Nirmal Kumar Bose (1901–1972)

Books in English

Cultural Anthropology. Calcutta: Arya Sahitya Bhavan; 2nd revised edition *Cultural Anthropology and Other Essays*. Calcutta: Indian Publishing Co., 1953.

Canons of Orissan Architecture. Calcutta: R. Chatterjee, 1932.

Studies in Gandhism. Calcutta: Merit Publishers, 1940.

Gandhiji's Theory of Trusteeship. Calcutta: Bangiya Pradeshik Chatra Samsad, 1946.

An Introduction to Gandhism. Calcutta: Bangiya Pradeshik Chatra Samsad, 1946.

Excavation at Mayurbhanj. Calcutta: University of Calcutta, 1948.

Satya and Ahimsa: Mahatma Gandhi's Interpretation. Calcutta: Committee for World Pacifist Meeting Pamphlets, 1949,

My Days with Gandhi. Calcutta: Merit Publications, 1953.

Modern Bengal. Calcutta: Vidyodaya Library, 1959.

Gandhiji: The Man and his Mission. Bombay: Bharatiya Vidya Bhavan, 1966.

Gandhi in Indian Politics. Bombay: Lalvani Publishing House, 1967.

Culture and Society in India. Calcutta: Asia Publishing House, 1967.

Problems of National Integration. Shimla: Indian Institute of Advanced Study, 1967.

A Study of Satyagraha. Poona: Poona University, 1968.

Calcutta: 1964: A Social Survey. Bombay: Lalvani Publishing House, 1968.

The Problems of Indian Nationalism. Bombay: Allied Publishers, 1969.

Gandhism in Modern India. Gauhati: Gauhati University, 1970.

Assam in Ahom Age, 1228–1826. Calcutta: Sanskrit Pustak Bhandar, 1970.

Lectures on Gandhism. Ahmedabad: Navajivan Publishing House, 1971.

Tribal Life in India. New Delhi: National Book Trust, 1971.

Anthropology and Some Indian Problems. Calcutta: Institute of Social Research and Applied Anthropology, 1972.

Indian Temple Designs. Calcutta: R. N. Bose, 1981.

Books in Bengali

Konaraker Bibaran (Description of Konark). Calcutta: Brahmo Mission Press, 1933; 2nd revised edition Purogami Prakashan, Calcutta, 1960.

Nabin o Prachin (The New and the Old). Calcutta: Arya Sahitya Bhavan, 1930; 2nd revised and enlarged edition Bengal Publishers, Calcutta, 1949.

Paribrajaker Diary (A Wanderer's Diary). Calcutta: D. M. Library, 1940; 2nd revised edition Vidyodaya Library, 1959; 1st Punascha edition Punascha, Calcutta, 2007.

Hindu Samajer Garan. Calcutta: Visvabharati, 1949; translated by André Béteille as *The Structure of Hindu Society*. New Delhi: Orient Longman, 1975.

Biallisher Bangla (Bengal of 1942). Calcutta: Saraswat Library, 1970.

Satchallisher Diary (Diary of 1947) edited by Abhik Kumar Dey. Calcutta: Punashcha, 2008.

Ganatantrer Sankat (Crisis of Democracy) edited by Abhra Ghosh. Calcutta: Sutradhar, 2013.

Edited Books

Selections from Gandhi. Ahmedabad: Navajivan Trust, 1934.

Social and Political Ideas of Mahatma Gandhi. New Delhi: Indian Council of World Affairs, 1949.

Peasant Life in India: A Study in Indian Unity and Diversity. Delhi: Government of India, Manager of Publications, 1961.

The Aryan Occupation of India. Calcutta: Indian Studies: Past and Present, 1962.

Data on Caste in Orissa. Calcutta: Anthropological Survey of India, 1962.

Studies in Indian Anthropology. Calcutta: Indian Studies: Past and Present, 1966.

Other Collections

Culture and Society in India and Other Essays. Kolkata: Chhatim Books, 2016.

Ramkrishna Mukherjee (1917–2015)

Books in English

(With co-authors) *Famine and Rehabilitation in Bengal*. Calcutta: Statistical Publishing Society, 1946.

(With C. R. Rao and J. C. Trevor) *The Physical Characteristics of the Ancient Inhabitants of Jebel Moya, Sudan*. Cambridge: Cambridge University Press, 1955.

The Problem of Uganda. Berlin: Akademie Verlag, 1956; 2nd revised edition *Uganda: An Historical Accident?* Trenton, New Jersey: Africa World Press, 1985.

The Dynamics of a Rural Society. Berlin: Akademie Verlag, 1957.

The Rise and Fall of the East India Company. Bombay: Popular Prakashan, 1958.

The Sociologist and Social Change in India Today. New Delhi: Prentice-Hall, 1965.

Six Villages in Bengal. Bombay: Popular Prakashan, 1971.

Social Indicators. Delhi: Macmillan and Co., 1975.

Family and Planning in India. New Delhi: Orient Longman, 1976.

West Bengal Family Structures: An Example of Vitality of Joint Family. New Delhi: Macmillan and Co., 1977.

What Will It Be? Explorations in Inductive Sociology. Bombay: Allied Publishers, 1979.

Sociology of Indian Sociology. Bombay: Allied Publishers, 1979.

Classifications in Social Research. Albany: State University of New York, 1983.

The Quality of Life: Valuation in Social Research. New Delhi: SAGE, 1989.

Society, Culture, Development. New Delhi: SAGE, 1991.

The Planning Problematic: The Role of Institutional Planning. New Delhi: Segment, 1991.

Systematic Sociology. New Delhi: SAGE, 1993.

The Measure of Time in the Appraisal of Social Reality. New Castle upon Tyne, UK: Cambridge Scholars Publishing, 2009.

Why Unitary Social Science? New Castle upon Tyne, UK: Cambridge Scholars Publishing, 2009.